New Spirituality, Self, and Belonging

Recent Titles in
Religion in the Age of Transformation

New Spirituality, Self, and Belonging

How New Agers and Neo-Pagans Talk about Themselves

Jon P. Bloch

Religion in the Age of Transformation

Anson Shupe, Series Adviser

PRAEGER

Westport, Connecticut
London

Library of Congress Cataloging-in-Publication Data

Bloch, Jon P.
    New spirituality, self, and belonging : how New Agers and Neo-Pagans talk about themselves / Jon P. Bloch.
        p.   cm.—(Religion in the age of transformation, ISSN 1087–2388)
    Includes bibliographical references and index.
    ISBN 0–275–95957–0 (alk. paper)
    1. New Age persons—Psychology—Case studies. 2. Neopagans—Psychology—Case studies. 3. New Age movement—Social aspects.
    4. Neopaganism—Social aspects. 5. New Age persons—Interviews.
    6. Neopagans—Interviews. I. Title. II. Series.
    BP605.N48B57   1998
    299'.93—dc21   97–27929

British Library Cataloguing in Publication Data is available.

Library of Congress Catalog Card Number: 97–27929
ISBN: 0–275–95957–0
ISSN: 1087–2388

First published in 1998

Praeger Publishers, 88 Post Road West, Westport, CT 06881
An imprint of Greenwood Publishing Group, Inc.

Printed in the United States of America

The paper used in this book complies with the Permanent Paper Standard issued by the National Information Standards Organization (Z39.48–1984).

10 9 8 7 6 5 4 3 2 1

Copyright Acknowledgment

The author and publisher gratefully acknowledge permission for use of the following material:

Excerpts from Richard Smolley, "Editorial." *Gnosis* No. 36 (Summer 1995): page 1. Reprinted by permission of Richard Smolley.

Contents

Introduction

"Alternative" or "countercultural" spirituality is comprised of eclectic assortments of world religious traditions, pop psychology, and the occult. Some of these beliefs or practices are called "New Age," involving alleged "parapsychological" activities, such as mediums or guided meditation. Other practices are deemed "Neo-Pagan," in that alleged spiritual powers are utilized to enact change, often through ritual or the occult (Melton and Moore 1982; Melton et al. 1990). But often these distinctions are useful more to social scientists than to alternative spiritualists themselves. Collectively, New Age and Neo-Paganism suggest both introspective and social needs, and often are combined in people's personalized belief systems, as well as in group-level activities or popular literature catering to these interests. Many of the people who participate in these activities do not dwell on whether what they are doing is "New Age" or "Neo-Pagan," and are not interested in such distinctions. In fact, often they prefer not to label their spirituality, even as it involves much of their discretionary time and money.

Thus, people refer to their pursuits as "spiritual" rather than as a form of "religion," for the latter terminology is more associated with distinctly organized groups who profess belief in a formalized doctrine. And such is not the case with countercultural spirituality. From one individual to the next, there are marked differences in beliefs and practices. Person A might practice Zen Buddhism, consult a Tarot card reader, and be studying Native American wisdom. Person B might be an astrologer who also studies the Christian-based "Course in Miracles" and is planning on attending a workshop on witchcraft. In fact, diversity is largely what makes this type of spirituality "alternative" or "countercultural." For alternative spiritualists are at odds with what is perceived to be the over-rationalization of mainstream society. Newer forms of social networks are sought that minimize organizational structure, hierarchy, or dogma, and instead emphasize self-autonomy (Bailey 1978; Misra and Preston 1978; Stone 1978; Neitz 1994).

In countercultural spirituality, the self is considered the final authority as to what to practice or believe. It is asserted that each person must find his or her particularized spiritual path to follow. One way to get alternative spiritualists *not* to listen to spiritual information is to present it dogmatically, as the "best" or "only" means to attain spiritual understanding.

Yet however loosely structured these clusters of individuals are, and however diverse the beliefs from one individual to the next, they consider themselves to be a "community." In fact, when meeting with these people, or perusing popular magazines that cater to such a readership, one encounters considerable emphasis on the importance of this community.

Therefore, on the one hand, countercultural spirituality offers the individual considerable latitude insofar as constructing a highly personalized spiritual belief system unlikely to be exactly like anyone else's. On the other hand, it offers a potent sense of social solidarity. Over the past few years, I have tried to learn how this seeming paradox works: What sorts of overriding shared beliefs or values provide Person A and Person B with a sense of community?

This book is about what I have uncovered to answer this question. It contains information from popular spiritual magazines, and observations from my field studies of large-scale and small group activities. But foremost, it features excerpts from in-depth interviews with a network of alternative spiritualists. The spoken word is a primary means by which religious or spiritual understanding is formulated and advanced (Fenn 1980; Stromberg 1993; Szuchewycz 1994; Wuthnow 1994), so I wanted to hear how people actually discussed their beliefs in detail and at length, and to assume as little as possible in advance. Given the diversity one encounters across countercultural spiritualists, it seemed necessary to elicit nuanced, personalized accounts to uncover and convey the social complexities involved in the paradox between self-autonomy and community.

Sociological literature to date on alternative forms of spirituality has tended to focus on relatively formalized groups, as indeed such groups exist. However, experience led me to conclude that a focus on a specific group would be somewhat misleading insofar as conveying the full character of countercultural spirituality. For example, from attending a weekly spiritual study group, I found no discernible social pressure to attend the group from one week to the next. Whether one attended regularly or sporadically, one was made to feel welcome, and one's comments were regarded as valid. Group attendance was not considered a measure as to the extensiveness of one's commitment to spirituality. Visiting the group from one week to the next could be a considerably different experience, depending on who was there.

Of equal importance, there were people who did not attend group meetings at all yet were talked about for having been in some other group. Though not physically present, these people whom "everyone knew" were important participants in the spiritual networks of those who technically *were* gathered. Participation in this group was at a relatively low social cost insofar as participating in other kinds of spiritual activities. In fact, information on activities of other groups was always permitted; there was little if any sense of competition between this group and other alternative spiritual activities.

In any case, whoever was present on a given evening did not necessarily practice the same things, or even have the same spiritual interpretation of key issues. For example, one evening the discussion centered around the topic of life after death. Some people stated that they believed in a Judeo-Christian concept of heaven. Others affirmed belief in reincarnation. Still others asserted that nothing happened after death, that we ultimately are but "worm food." In the end, someone suggested that whatever one believed happened to the self upon dying would be what happened, that multiple realities were possible. For all the diversity that had been expressed, the group had no problem agreeing to this.

Other nights (in this group and others I observed) found differences of opinion fully tolerated on theological issues such as monotheism or "spirit guides," as well as social topics such as capital punishment, transsexualism, and whether or not men and women are "born different" from each other. Even when it came to group activities such as guided meditations or "psychic" exercises, people would describe very different results. Some claimed to have had deeply meaningful experiences, while others claimed to have experienced little.

Turning to large-scale activities, often sponsored by an umbrella group ("membership" to which generally consisted of being on a mailing list), I encountered a similar situation. At fairs and festivals, booths and tables offered such diverse services as massage therapy, Tarot card readings, numerology charts, astrological charts, Reiki (a form of spiritual healing), and medium consultation (including past life "recalls" and futuristic predictions). Others offered artifacts such as crystals, tribal-like drums, or handmade Celtic runes (another form of oracular consultation). Workshops focused on such topics as yoga, meditation techniques (from numerous Hindu, Buddhist or contemporary traditions), tribal dancing or drumming, or Tai Chi. Lectures were given on various occult practices, or on matters such as learning to get in touch with guardian angels.

None of this varied information was presented in a spirit of competition or contradiction. If one wanted to take up Zen meditation at noon and then an hour later pursue the "Course in Miracles," so doing was considered to be a valid pursuit in order to find what aspects of what teaching best suited the self. Fundamentally, all information was considered equal, expressing but different manifestations of the same overriding spiritual condition of life. Information was offered free or with a nominal charge; sometimes, trade was the only form of currency permitted at tables.

Even blatant contradictions were considered unimportant. For example, at a weekend of spiritual workshops, Speaker A stated that there were twelve "spirit guides" in the cosmos, while Speaker B stated that there were 4,000. When I asked persons whom I saw at both events what they thought of this apparent contradiction, four of them replied with words to the effect that what the one speaker meant by spirits could be different from what the other speaker meant. A fifth individual said she had not noticed the contradiction and did not know what to make of it. Another person found the contradiction humorous, and freely admitted he often was skeptical of information presented at these events, but stated that on balance he still felt that spirituality was worth pursuing.

Popular magazines offer advertisements and articles that reflected this tolerance for diversity. For example, the July/August 1996 issue of *New Age Journal* (circulation 240,000) reveals ads for Chinese herbal healing, astrology, spiritual healing, shamanism, Native American spirituality, futuristic prediction, Tibetan Buddhism, and card readings. There is a feature on John Dugdale, a photographer with AIDS losing his eyesight yet still actively taking pictures, and who describes his spirituality as one that "folds Tibetan Buddhist practice into staunch Episcopalianism, then stirs in a vigorous animism" (Oliver 1996:89). Other articles cover topics such as Benedictine monasteries, popular psychology, yoga and "plant shamanism." Presumably, *New Age Journal* is targeted toward a particular readership, yet it is not based on any singular affiliation.

In fact, there are anywhere from 83,000 to 333,000 persons in the U.S. who might be considered "Neo-Pagan" at present, yet probably only about ten percent of these people belong to an organized group (Melton et al. 1990; Kelly 1992). Existing literature has not fully explored how this flight away from organization while emphasizing self-autonomy paradoxically suggests new models of community. By exploring a cluster of individuals who on Tuesday night gather together as "Zen Buddhists," one is not considering that several of them are "Wiccans" on a different night of the week. Moreover, one is not addressing the fact that these people more accurately regard themselves as seeking spiritual experience and understanding outside of mainstream social institutions, and at present happen to be exploring both Zen and Wicca. It is this fundamental, overriding countercultural spiritual identity and community that I attempt to define.

By focusing on in-depth interviews, I also hope to offer more information as to how these people actually go about "making sense" of the things they believe: How do people reckon between working nine-to-five and holding highly idealized views as to the "true" spiritual nature of life? For all the emphasis as to *why* people turn to New Age or Neo-Paganism, there has not been enough study as to *how* people who believe in things like psychic phenomena, Tarot card readings or Goddess worship actually go about formulating these beliefs when discussing the life experience.

Some readers might find the assertions offered by the people I interviewed difficult to accept, but they serve a very ordinary function in people's lives: to obtain a sense of direction and purpose, as well as some measure of understanding as to why things happen as they do. Other readers might decide some of the ideas these people advance are contradictory or impractical. Like anyone else, alternative spiritualists hold to certain beliefs, and like anyone else, some of these beliefs suggest more utility than others. Again like anyone else, sometimes these individuals are not able to live up to their beliefs, or suffer frustration or disappointment that their beliefs are not adequate to a particular situation.

But much of the time, they are able to find ways of discussing their spirituality as it applies to their daily lives in ways that "make sense": What they believe in the abstract seems adequate to explain what happens empirically. Hastily, some might assume that no one in his or her "right mind" possibly could believe in things like past-life recall, or drumming as a spiritual pursuit. But as I was to discover, such individuals virtually never stop thinking about the so-called "real" world: how to improve it, and how to feel a happier and more successful part of it. The struggle to maintain a spiritual understanding of life when contrasted with the harshness of secular reality is all but ceaseless. These people work, go to school, pay their taxes, and raise their children. Yet they also would appear to be highly introspective individuals who seek and often find highly-nuanced spiritual meanings from even the smallest everyday occurrence.

In Chapter 1, I construct a model for analysis of the interviews. I argue that alternative spirituality can be viewed as a contemporary social movement, in that it utilizes ideology to create new symbolic communication codes to attack mainstream social controls and promote its minority perspective, even as it does not formally engage in overt political action. Whatever the topic being discussed, it is possible to frame it from an alternative spiritual perspective, whereby this perspective dominates one's worldview and continues to be featured in the presence of competing secular and/or institutionalized religious claims.

Subsequent chapters are largely based upon this model, and are divided into common themes and concerns across interviewees that indicate the presence of a shared community, despite individual differences in practices or beliefs. In Chapter 2, I analyze ideological declarations made in interviews that concerned the strain between self-autonomy and community, and how these strains were resolved in ways that favored the alternative spiritual viewpoint. In Chapter 3, I note instances in which interviewees ideologically addressed the symbolic epistemological strain between matter and spirit, as specifically expressed in the strain between scientific and spiritual ways of understanding. Mainstream forms of knowledge were subsumed within an alternative spiritual frame of reference. Chapter 4 consists of other common strains concerning matter and spirit: conceptualizing the earth as sacred along with the sky-like "heavens," honoring the image of the female goddess along with the male god, and valuing darkness as sacred (instead of evil) along with symbolic images of light. Alternative spirituality was viewed by interviewees as providing a full range of spiritual experience, as opposed to competing explanations that honor only the sky, the male, and the light.

Chapter 5 contains instances in which interviewees discussed limitations in their belief systems, personalities, or group activities, but in ways that still featured and affirmed alternative spirituality. In Chapter 6, I discuss how different kinds of comments made during interviews suggested elements of the mythic, whereby these comments were asserted to be all the more compelling or meaningful. The Conclusion contains a brief summary and discussion of the findings, noting some of the paradoxical strengths and limitations of any ideological framework.

1

Conceptualizing Alternative Spirituality

This chapter advances a framework for analyzing the in-depth interviews with twenty-two alternative spiritualists that are the focus of this book. I locate the countercultural spiritual movement within a framework of larger social currents. I offer a brief description of how the sample was constructed and describe each of the interviewees, to illustrate how these alternative spiritualists reflect these large-scale social imperatives. The chapter concludes with a theoretical conceptualization of this phenomenon, and a methodological means for applying it.

ALTERNATIVE SPIRITUALITY AS A SOCIAL PHENOMENON

Alternative spiritualists find little need to share an organized creed or belief system, and instead emphasize personal experience, and the right of each individual to seek for himself or herself what to practice and believe (Bailey 1978; Misra and Preston 1978; Stone 1978; Adler 1986; Melton et al. 1990; Kelly 1992; Neitz 1994). The relatively fluid networks that characterize countercultural spirituality reflect larger social trends and dilemmas in contemporary society. Current society often is characterized by a paradoxical strain between the need for self-autonomy and solidarity ties with others based on shared normative expectations.

Industrialization increased possibilities for class mobility, travel, and access to diverse information. Consequently, individuals began to feel relatively unconstrained to make more life choices for themselves. Also, with access to more social possibilities there evolved a paramount sense of each person having a "unique" self (Durkheim 1951; Turner 1976; Gagnon 1992). As noted by Simmel (1955:140), while some groups make stronger claims upon certain individuals, people nonetheless maintain multiple group affiliations. The more group affiliations one has, "the more improbable it is that other persons will exhibit the same combinations of group affiliations, that these particular groups will 'intersect' once again [in a second individual]." An individual's unique intersection of group affiliations provides self-definition (Simmel 1955:141): "[T]he person . . . regains his individuality, because his pattern of participation is unique; hence the fact of multiple group participation creates in turn a new subjective element . . . Hence, individuality [becomes] interpreted as that particular set of constituent elements which in their quality and combination make up the individual."

The "unique" bundle of social expectations that one refers to as one's "individuality" has been viewed as something only the self can explore or evaluate; outsiders could not have full access to or understanding of this unique personage. Previously, society had been considered the force that provided definition for self-identity, but now there was a trend toward the opposite view: that society, with its laws and normative restrictions, often was an obstacle to self-fulfillment. One might have to take actions that violated social expectations in order to realize "true" selfhood (Durkheim 1951; Simmel 1955; Turner 1976; Gagnon 1992).

The religious domain has not been invulnerable to this trend toward individualism. Luckmann (1967:103) discusses the advent of "invisible religion," in which the locus of authority as to what to believe was within the self, and religion became an "invisible" pursuit for this emphasis on self-autonomy:

> The social form of religion emerging in modern industrial societies is characterized by the direct accessibility of an assortment of religious representations to potential consumers. The sacred cosmos is mediated neither through a specialized domain of religious institutions nor through other primary public institutions. It is the direct accessibility of the sacred cosmos, more precisely, through an assortment of religious themes, which makes religion today essentially a phenomenon of the "private sphere."

Luckmann locates religious shifts within a framework of shifting social organization. In tribal or agrarian societies, the social order is relatively concrete and direct (as exemplified through the kinship structure), whereby the individual's social actions and "self" are relatively unified. Primary socialization in non-modernized societies essentially teaches the individual all one needs to know about the "self." By contrast, modern society sees greater segmentation and differentiation. One's worldview becomes less unitary — and less obligatory. No single knowledge claim or organization has a clear monopoly; competing worldviews will be added to those received in primary socialization. The one overriding social "institution" is no longer an institution at all; rather, it is the individual. Persons exposed to a multiplicity of competing religious claims will decide for themselves as "consumers" what to pick and choose from which belief system. Their ultimate loyalty or affinity is not as likely to be toward an organized group.

Moreover, an overriding desire to unify seemingly disparate worldviews has been conceptualized as integral to the contemporary life experience. Given the social uncertainty that can arise when bombarded with so much competing information, people often attempt to acknowledge numerous forms of understanding (religious and/or secular) with a minimum of contradiction to their overriding belief systems. In fact, contemporary pathology could be conceptualized as a fanatical *avoidance* of the multiplicity of worldviews that confront the individual in the information age (Luhmann 1982). In this context, someone's becoming a "Hindu Methodist" can seem a creative and functional solution for reducing social uncertainty.

Thus, alternative spirituality is but one of many permutations of a contemporary flight away from highly rationalized organizational structure. These individuals acquire combinations of social roles and expectations relatively unique to each individual, whereby one's sense of individuality is heightened. They enact a process of "self-discovery" that places the focus upon the self and away from social restrictions. Theirs is a consumerist and personalized approach to acquisition of religious or spiritual information. It is largely based on a desire to reduce social uncertainty by seeking compatibility across different knowledge claims, rather than having to select one at the absolute social cost of another.

But there is an element of irony here: While often taken for granted as an essential human condition, the desire to "find oneself" is dependent to a major extent upon social forces that articulate this possibility and enable it to occur—even as flight away from society paradoxically is sought (Durkheim 1951; Simmel 1955; Mead 1962; Turner 1976; Zurcher 1983; Gagnon 1992). These newer expressions of spirituality are "countercultural" within a larger social framework that permits these forms of dissension to occur, and in moderation perhaps even praises such efforts as being not antithetical to larger social principles (Barker 1993).

Furthermore, even when people are not aware of the extent to which their time and place are informing their sense of "individuality," they are aware of having needs for solidarity ties with others. One requires both personal identity and a shared history with others. And even one's personal "identity" involves normative expectations acquired from social forces and experiences outside the self. Hence, social institutions have needed to be developed that have seemed to offer a measure of self-autonomy and a simultaneous sense of community. There is a concurrent need to feel that there are beliefs or perceptions unique to the self, but also that one shares certain norms or beliefs with others (Durkheim 1951; Simmel 1955; Mead 1962; Turner 1976; Zurcher 1983; Gagnon 1992; Shotter 1993).

Thus, countercultural spiritualists appear to be seeking both the desire for self-autonomy as well as to reduce uncertainty through engaging in elements of the pre-modern social order (e.g., the appeal of eastern religions, or tribal rituals) to also feel that there is a community that they share values with, and which informs their sense of self. Interestingly, one of the fundamental shared beliefs across alternative spiritualists is the very importance of self-autonomy in modern society. For as already noted, this gravitation toward "nonconformity" paradoxically is a form of shared value in modern society as a whole.

Popular countercultural spiritual magazines reveal ample evidence of this movement toward self-autonomy while also maintaining a strong sense of community through a shared belief *concerning* this need for self-autonomy. For example, in *Llewellyn's New Worlds of Mind and Spirit*, Cicero and Cicero (1995:52) discussed the practice of "self-initiation," which "is a valid and effective alternative for today's spiritual seekers who want to progress at their own rate, without pressure from teacher, gurus or peers." Similarly, in a recent issue of *Yoga Journal*, Andrew Harvey (in an interview with Ingram, 1995) stated that the guru system is no longer useful, and that the time has come for each person to find his/her direct and unmediated relationship with spiritual forces. These authors emphasized self-autonomy, but discussed it in terms of being a shared social understanding and endeavor.

Perhaps even more to the point, the Summer 1995 issue of *Gnosis: A Journal of the Western Inner Traditions* (Smoley 1995: 1) had an editorial that read, in part, as follows (my italics, unless otherwise indicated):

> No issue on the Inner Planes would be complete without talking about the hidden brotherhood — those wise, almost omniscient figures who work in secret to further the evolution of humankind. . . . Are these individuals real or mythic — Do they exist in the flesh, hidden away in mountain fastnesses, or can they be found only in the realm of the imagination? Why do they stay out of view?
>
> Secret societies do exist. . . . Like all else in human life, they seem to span the range from the noblest to the basest of purposes. But I wouldn't say that these organizations, even the best of them taken *en masse* [author's italics], constitute the scattered brotherhood either.
>
> In fact, I'd say that the brotherhood (which is also a sisterhood) is secret precisely because *it can't be equated with any one organization*. . . Joining this brotherhood, I believe, isn't a matter of learning secret handshakes or mystical syllables. Instead it involves taking a conscious vow of responsibility for oneself and for the welfare of others, and offering allegiance, not to any particular religious form, but to *the ultimate, ineffable truth that underlies all forms*. At times, I'm sure, this is done in the context of a group, *but it can also be carried out privately, in one's own heart*. . . . And what is the goal of this society? Fulfilling the word of God? Advancing human evolution? Maybe. But . . . the ordinary world provides enough of these agendas already. Rather it seems that this acknowledgment of *a truth beyond all creeds* constitutes the brotherhood's goal as well as its starting point, furnishing its members with *a common life that undercuts any differences in belief*. As Heraclitus

said, "Those who are awake all live in the same world. Those who are asleep live in their own worlds."

In brief, it would appear that the alternative spiritual social network finds solidarity in being something of a "secret" that "can't be equated with any one organization." Its relative lack of hierarchy or dogma simultaneously provides shared spiritual meaning and a paradoxical unity. Perhaps this is why the "Reader's Survey" in a recent issue of *Green Egg: A Journal of the Awakening Earth* (1995:39) listed the following choices for present religious affiliation: Pagan, Wiccan, Goddess Spirituality, Buddhist, Agnostic/Atheist, New Age, Unitarian, Jewish, Eclectic, and "other."[1]

Not only did this survey suggest a target readership geared at diverse spiritual ties, but the very labels themselves can be somewhat ambiguous. For it is a matter of how one defines the self. What Person A calls "Pagan" is not necessarily what Person B calls it. Some might use terms such as "Pagan" or "Wiccan" interchangeably, while others do not. Some people might employ aspects of Goddess spirituality in their beliefs but not label themselves a Goddess worshipper. (And it is interesting to note that the respect for diverse perceptions of reality is such that "Atheist/Agnostic" was one of the choices.[2])

However, while meanings can be idiosyncratically personalized, they are not necessarily mutually exclusive, and can still indicate shared meanings, whereby group information and self-conceptualization overlap (Brewer 1993; Wuthnow 1994). While Person A and Person B might have varying ideas as to what it means to be a "Pagan" or a "Goddess Worshipper," there is likely to be partial agreement — or at very least enough commonalty to comprehend what the other person means by a given term.

Just as important, there is at least some overlap across individuals as to the components of a personalized spiritual belief system, as well as certain overriding values or beliefs. The latter includes flight from singular belief systems, or highly rationalized organizations, for their alleged limitations. This is illustrated by briefly discussing the twenty-two people I assembled to be interviewed.

DIVERSITY AND COMMONALITY: CONSTRUCTING A SAMPLE

Given that countercultural spiritualists characteristically construct personalized and highly nuanced belief systems, I anticipated interviewing people with open-ended questions that would permit more personalized and nuanced answers. Therefore, I purposefully constructed a relatively small sample size. Through my fieldwork at large- and small-scale events, I established social ties with a number of individuals.[3] Eleven of these people became part of my ultimate sample of twenty-two. Another eleven individuals were persons whom I had not met before, but who responded to ads I placed in strategic locations (such as an occult bookstore, and a nature sanctuary that hosts large-scale spiritual events). Half the interviewees were male, half were female. The age range was from early twenties to about fifty, therefore including persons who had been pursuing alternative spirituality since the late sixties/early seventies, as well as persons who had been doing so for only a few years. Thus, though the sample was largely one of convenience, efforts were made to safeguard against unintended biases by gender, age or personal familiarity. (See also Table 1.1.)

Table 1.1: Profile of Sample

Profile of Sample	N=22	Percent of Sample
Male	11	50
Female	11	50
Age 20-29	10	45
Age 30-39	8	36
Age 40-49	4	18
European-American	22	100
Marital Status		
Married	3	14
Cohabiting	1	5
Single	18	82
Divorced	6	27
Widowed	1	5
Has Children	6	27
Education		
Undergraduate Student	5	23
Graduate Student	2	9

Profile of Sample	N=22	Percent of Sample
Bachelor's Degree (highest level)	5	23
Master's Degree (highest level)	3	14
Some College	5	23
High School (highest level)	2	9
Employment		
Professional/White Collar	4	18
Service/Clerical	4	18
Self-Employed	7	32
Full time Student	7	32
Religious Background		
Raised Catholic	8	36
Raised Protestant	8	36
Raised Catholic and Protestant	1	5
Raised No Religion	5	23

Collectively, these people either knew each other or else knew many of the same people. It would not be unlikely to see them all at the same event. Yet no two individuals gave indication of having the precise same configuration of spiritual beliefs. Thus, this collection of individuals was suggestive of exactly the type of spiritual network that would seem to be emblematic of countercultural spirituality. Here are these twenty-two individuals:

Maria

An artist and returning student in her thirties,[4] Maria applied her love of art to her spirituality. She made ritual tools from various religious traditions, such as icons or tribal rattles. When praying or meditating at her bedside at night, she sometimes used the Catholic prayers of her childhood, or the "Serenity Prayer" from the twelve-step programs. However, if Maria had the energy, she created her own prayers, which might involve Native American singing, drumming and rattling. Tapes on dream interpretation by a prominent Jungian analyst were important to her spirituality, as were activities such as rebirthing, and books on eastern philosophy. Maria discussed in detail certain forms of highly mystical, psychic or "out-of-body" experiences she believed to have experienced. She also had actively pursued feminist spirituality, and expressed deep concern for the environment in a spiritual context.

Jack

A graduate student in his twenties, Jack also grew up Catholic,[5] but found it difficult to reckon between his life experiences and what his religion was teaching him. He also felt it did not satisfactorily address world problems such as war or pollution. He began to study pamphlets on reincarnation, which became an important aspect of his spiritual beliefs. This set in motion exposure to Goddess spirituality and Wicca, along with the Arthurian legends (which he viewed as spiritual). However, many of his spiritual practices stemmed from Hinduism: Jack practiced meditation and Kundalini, and performed a "cleansing" of the spiritual energy centers, or chakras, along his body. Yet this process also involved songs and vocal tones of Native American spirituality. Jack also had been studying the tarot and had four different decks reflecting various cultural traditions.

Gypsy

Though not raised within a strong religious tradition, Gypsy, a librarian in her twenties, had a family that encouraged her to explore different religions on her own. Disliking the limited roles that women were permitted in mainline Christian denominations, she gravitated to books on witchcraft and feminist spirituality. However, ultimately Gypsy felt that spirituality must transcend gender in order for all people to work together. As for witchcraft, she reconfigured it through additional sources such as Native American spirituality and tantric-based sources. Ultimately, Gypsy developed what she considered her triple-based approach to spirituality: dream work ritual, dance ritual and tantric-influenced sex magic. She frequently participated in earth-based spiritual events.

Jerry

The concept of a punishing God (as expressed within the Catholic tradition he was raised in) did not appeal to Jerry (a shopkeeper in his thirties). He found he felt a sense of spirituality in the woods that his religion did not talk about — and which told him it was "the devil playing tricks" with him. Jerry developed what he considered to be his own, personalized religion stemming from numerous different Pagan and shamanistic traditions (including Native American), and was willing to participate in any number of group activities thereof. But Jerry also considered simply being in the woods and following the cycles of nature to be a spiritual activity, along with anything he might do that is connected to the protection of the natural environment (i.e., planting a tree, recycling, picking up trash in the woods).

Laurel

At about age six, Laurel, a returning student in her thirties, asked to go to church, but she and her family grew "bored with it really fast." Having always had experiences she defined as psychic or clairvoyant, she was exposed to tribal medicine ways and voodoo; she also began to study Jungian concepts of mythological archetypes. Next, Laurel got involved with "a sort of experimental, eclectic magical group" that used the Kabbala as a basis for many of their rituals. She then met with a group that pursued Native American spirituality. Much of her spiritual activity at present centered around the study of color. For example, burning a particular color of candle was used to effect a particular change within her life. She meditated, worked with animal guides, and was exploring parallels between totemism and the chakras. Laurel also used astrology, the tarot, and magic-related artifacts such as a wand, sword and staff. She felt that books on the Native American medicine cards and Carlos Castanada's books about his spiritual visions were helpful as well.

Steven

Out of anyone I interviewed, Steven, an artist in his thirties, came closest to having a spiritual belief system that firmly accepted or rejected certain information. "As you can see, I'm somewhat opinionated." In fact, he belongs to one of the more organized groups in the Neo-Pagan community. Interested in mythology, science fiction, and fantasy even as a child, Steven had been rigorously pursuing his spirituality through this organization for the past six years. However, the spiritual program he followed included elements of eastern spirituality such as yoga. Steven also participated in largely improvised rituals and festivals, such as celebrations of the earth. The spiritual tools of his choice are "more or less western with a couple of extras," and "tend to be kind of eclectic." In fact, Steven felt that the best spiritual tools were ones people made for themselves. He once spent two years crafting a series of magical tools based on his understanding of the twelve months of the year and the twelve signs of the zodiac. Other people I interviewed stated that the deity(s) of different religions were fundamentally representative of similar spiritual forces, but Steven believed that the different deities were literal and distinct beings, and that "the idea of monotheism betokens, for one thing, a distinct lack of imagination."

Arthur

A returning student in his thirties, Arthur was raised in a conservative Protestant religion. Rebellion led him to pursue (as both student and teacher) earth-based spiritual festivals, a wide spectrum of psychic and dream experiences, and numerous forms of ceremonial magic across various traditions. For example, Arthur discussed the interconnection between the twenty-two paths contained within the Kabbalistic Tree of Life with the tarot. In telling the story of how he met a significant other, he referred to evoking the presence of the "Sumerian Babylonian Goddess of Ishtar." A private altar in Arthur's home featured an eclectic assortment of artifacts across spiritual traditions that were intended to invoke a wide range of spiritual forces. There, he enacted meditative, psychic, and ceremonial rituals to increase his personal sense of spirituality.

Anthony

When the parents of Anthony, a school teacher in his forties, divorced when he was a child, he had difficulty accepting the Catholic teaching that his parents would have to suffer for their "sin." As he was already having dreams that portended some other realm of spirituality, he began to study various forms of Wiccan and occult traditions. Eventually, he focused largely on voodoo rituals and belief systems. However, his significant other was a Tibetan Buddhist, so he also studied and practiced spiritual techniques from this other discipline. He found no contradiction between the two, but rather felt that they "come together" for him. Moreover, Anthony was open-minded about participating in ceremonies and rituals across different traditions. For example, he talked about a powerful experience he had while participating in a Native American sweat lodge with a shaman. He also considered daily life actions that benefited others, such as teaching his students, or recycling, to be spiritual activities.

Larry

A drama teacher in his twenties, Larry to some extent still considered himself the Lutheran he was raised to be — or, more accurately, a "radical Lutheran anarchist." He studied ritual magic, shamanic forms of healing (including Native American), mythology for inner growth (as per Joseph Campbell and others), and employed elements of Zen Buddhism his "own way." Larry also felt that his way of living was in agreement with Hinduism, "particularly the Bhagavad Gita." Additionally, he studied Taoism, stated that he had had numerous psychic experiences, and (as a teacher of theater) also considered music and drama to be an integral part of his spiritual expression. Indeed, Larry utilized his theatrical training in group settings, helping to organize or improvise rituals. He felt that people working together to save the earth was a highly spiritual endeavor, and also considered the philosophical concept of "paradox" as elaborated by authors such as Wittgenstein to be integral to his conceptualization of spirituality.

Clarissa

Though raised Catholic, Clarissa, a college student in her twenties, "just sort of went through the motions" and was more or less an atheist until she discovered feminist spirituality. From this tradition, she developed a deepened sense of respect for the earth, and considered all life forms connected to "the same vital energy." Therefore, Clarissa believed that seemingly small actions such as recycling have spiritual significance in her life. She participated in goddess-based lunar rituals, followed lunar charts, and had experienced what is called "soul retrieval," which she described as an ancient, shamanic-based tradition. Clarissa believed she was able to communicate with spiritual life forms, and also found spiritual meaning from her dreams and from ritualistic drumming. Drawing largely from the Native American tradition, she used crystals, incense, the burning of sage, and "dream-catchers" (which have helped her to have more vivid dreams). She also studied and used the tarot.

Ralph

A dishwasher in his twenties, Ralph disliked the racism, patriarchal bias, and lack of attention paid to the earth that he experienced in the Catholicism of his upbringing. His introduction to alternative spirituality came largely through drumming. After participating in drumming circles at Grateful Dead concerts, Ralph started to feel that there was more to this tradition than the music per se: that it was possible to get "naturally high without the use of drugs, you know what I mean — and just play our inner rhythm." In addition to drumming, Ralph talked quite a lot about healing and getting in touch with the earth, in ways suggestive of Native Americanism. But in his regular attendance at spiritual festivals, Ralph participated in ritual and magic circles of whatever variety. He also believed in guardian angels, the earth as a spiritual force, and elected to address the higher power of his understanding as "Lord."

Alex

A student in her twenties, Alex began to explore the possibility of there being a "universal pattern" to all things while still in high school, though she was not raised in any particular religious tradition. This exploration led to a discovery of feminist, earth-based spirituality, mythology (especially the ancient goddess religions), astrology, the Merlin stone, magic, and the moon cycles, as well as books by authors such as Ram Das. Alex felt an especially strong spiritual presence while being in the forest with like-minded "magical" people. While she enjoyed doing tarot readings, her earth-based activities such as gardening were considered to be spiritual unto themselves.

Flora

A massage therapist in her twenties, Flora was raised Catholic, and for a time became a conservative Christian. She had since become an active participant in spiritual festivals, and has pursued a wide range of spiritual topics. These have included the earth elements, chakras, psychic energy, drum circles, reincarnation, magic and Shamanism across traditions (including eastern and Native American), along with vision questing, spiritual healing, body work, meditation and the goddess archetypes.

Badger

Raised in Catholicism, Badger grew impatient with that doctrine for what he perceived to be its lack of knowledge about karma and its disconnectedness from the earth. He talked about what he called "spiritual farming," and the need to respect the interconnectedness of all life forms. He practiced yoga and Reiki, meditated, and participated in Native American rituals. Badger believed in dream messages and magic, but he also stated that an important spiritual ritual could be "going down to the creek every day to take a bath."

Sylvia

A social worker in her thirties, Sylvia began having what she perceived to be psychic experiences at a very young age. Her Protestant church was disinclined to recognize them as valid. Interested in exploring concepts such as reincarnation and witchcraft, Sylvia decided against becoming ordained within her religion of origin. Instead, she studied books by feminist spiritual authors such as Starhawk and Margot Adler, and helped organize spirituality workshops and groups for women. She still found feminist spirituality valuable, but also felt a need to be inclusive of both genders. Sylvia's other long-term spiritual interests have included massage therapy, psychic healing, past life regression, spiritual and science fiction festivals, guided meditations, and chakra and aura cleansing, to which lattermost activity she had fused totemism. She also used the tarot and *I Ching*, as well as drums and other musical instruments as spiritual tools.

Eli

A returning student in his thirties, Eli was exposed to both Catholic and Protestant traditions while growing up. But by a fairly young age he began to study and be introduced to witchcraft, and preferred both the theory and the sense of community he found to either organized Christian group. Well-versed in "traditional" witchcraft, and having been exposed to Kabbalistic and other related traditions, Eli nonetheless designed his own rituals or enactments of magic. In so doing, he drew upon his knowledge of tradition as well as his spontaneous needs or feelings of the moment. Eli considered earth-based activities to be spiritual — even simple things like growing a houseplant. He also meditated, and stated that basic activities such as eating or having sex also were forms of witchcraft and magic.

Iris

Raised within conservative Protestantism, Iris, an accountant in her thirties, still appreciated the sense of community that this religious tradition sometimes gave her. Nonetheless, she had difficulty with the numerous rules and restrictions she felt were being imposed on her. After declaring herself an atheist while still attending a religious school, she began to experience what she called "gnosis," a sense of connectedness amongst all things that she began to view as spiritual. Over time, Iris exposed herself to a wide range of traditions and practices, and found an especial affinity for Native American shamanism, Kundalini yoga, Celtic runes, meditative breathing and stretching exercises, runes, and what she experienced as communication with otherworldly life forms. Iris did tarot readings with various decks, and used numerous spiritual tools (she finds her drum and rattle especially useful). She also considered earth-based pursuits such as gardening to be spiritual activities.

Edward

Self-described as an "inventor" in his thirties, Edward had been both scientifically and spiritually oriented for most of his life. This has led him to study the major religious traditions of the world, looking for ways of finding scientific "proof" for certain kinds of religious phenomena. Among the numerous spiritual sources he considered especially useful were yoga, Hinduism (including concepts such as reincarnation), Zen, Native American and other earth-based spiritual traditions, parts of the Bible, and psychic experiences involving activities such as healings and clairvoyance. Dream work also was important to Edward, along with scientific literature and significant works of fiction. For example, the authors that have most informed his spirituality included Castanada, Einstein and Shakespeare.

Melanie

The Episcopalianism of her family of origin did not sit well with Melanie, an office worker in her twenties. She found many of its practitioners hypocritical for what she perceived to be their materialistic, competitive, and sexist tendencies. Instead, she developed a strong feeling for nature as a spiritual force. Melanie followed the lunar cycles and based much of her spiritual practice and communication around the moon. She had a personal altar in her home at which she meditated daily, and performed private rituals with whatever implements she felt most comfortable using. Melanie also discussed having had psychic dream experiences. Much of her ritual enactment revolved around dance, and she also used feathers, herbs, flowers, jewelry, crystals, wands, and staffs as spiritual tools. Additionally, she felt it important to be well-versed in a variety of religious traditions, so that if people challenged her beliefs, she could articulate an informed response. Hence, Melanie read and studied the religious doctrines of Christianity, Judaism, Islam, and different forms of Buddhism.

Marcie

A small business owner in her forties, Marcie had a Protestant mother and an atheistic, scientist father. This led her to explore various belief systems from a young age. Over the years, she had studied and practiced Hinduism, various forms of meditation, Western European ceremonial magic, and voodoo. Marcie had read extensively into a variety of mythic traditions, including Hopi and Arthurian, and also had studied psychic phenomena. She had collected an assortment of spiritual symbols and icons, such as wands, words, cups, chalices, and statues of Kali and other spiritual entities — including the Virgin Mary. But Marcie also was striving for as broad a definition of "spirituality" as possible, and felt that daily actions related to the earth also were spiritual.

Mary Lou

A forty-one-year-old massage therapist, Mary Lou was rigorously exposed to both art and science while growing up, creating an interest in both science and creative forces that she eventually came to think of as spiritual. She believed that scientific information could be a form of spiritual understanding, and considered her library of books on science to be among her spiritual tools, along with her books on art. Besides meditation and an active exposure to a wide range of spiritual traditions such as Tai Chi, Native American earth-based rituals, magic, and various types of psychic activities, Mary Lou developed a form of massage therapy she considered highly spiritual. Besides touch, it involved certain kinds of music she found spiritually healing or illuminating, as well as herbs, oils, and fragrances used to elicit specific kinds of spiritual responses.

Jesse

A small business owner in his forties, Jesse was raised in mainline Protestantism, but it lacked relevance and meaning for him, as well as a sense of spiritual force. Over the years, Jesse had pursued witchcraft, meditation, circle casting, eastern philosophy, spiritual cleansing, shamanism, gnosticism, the Carlos Castanada books, and studies of the ancient elements as spiritual forces. He also maintained that science fiction, space exploration, and other forms of futuristic technology were part of his spirituality. Jesse claimed to have had numerous kinds of psychic or "out of body" experiences. Over the years, he had helped to organize various spiritual groups, activities, and enterprises. Currently, he was active in one of several groups in the vicinity that emphasized creating an atmosphere in which people could pursue diverse, eclectic and personalized configurations of spirituality.

As seen in Table 1.2, there was considerable overlap across interviewees, despite the fact that no two people had collected precisely the same assortment of beliefs and practices. Also, even when technical specifics varied, two different types of beliefs or experiences both suggested a sympathy for "psychic" phe-nomena or "eastern" thought. In addition to this overlap of beliefs, these indi-viduals often shared in common a disenchantment with their religion of origin over some perceived limitation it exhibited for being highly organized. Indeed, these individuals each seemed to practice an emergent spirituality, in which one was constantly open to new information. And as shall be seen in subse-quent chapters, there were other fundamental issues they had in common, such as a belief that the earth is spiritual.

Table 1.2: General Similarities of Belief and Practice

General Similarities of Belief and Practice	N=22	Percent of Sample
Psychic experiences (e.g., dreams, out-of-body, healing)	16	73
Magic (Shamanism, Kabbalism)	22	100
Eastern (Zen, Hinduism, yoga)	17	77
Native American tools and rituals	19	86
Other tools and oracles (tarot, runes, astrology)	18	82
Meditation	17	77
Earth as spiritual	22	100
Willing to participate in other kinds of spirituality	22	100
Disenchantment with organized religions	22	100

In sum, a glance across interviewees suggests both self-autonomy and a sense of community for certain shared attitudes. This was to become even more apparent when I collected and analyzed the interviews with these people, so much so that collectively the interviews indicated complex yet discernible pro-cesses that required sociological clarification.

IDEOLOGY, SYMBOLIC CAPITAL, AND SOCIAL MOVEMENTS

The mutual needs for self-autonomy and community can be conceptualized as a form of social *strain*. Geertz discussed how Parsons and others (see Gieryn 1983:782) have noted that ideological declarations "are symptoms — as well as symbolic resolutions — of role strain, contradiction and disequalibrium." Hence, "strain" here connotes both the contradictory condition itself, and the symbolic reckoning with it. Potentially, one could offer that (for example) the articles from *Llewellyn's* or *Yoga Journal* concerned a symbolic strain between self-autonomy and the spiritual tradition of the guru — resulting in the alleged trend toward "self-initiation." Both pronounced the existence of a strain between self and group tradition, as well as conceptualized a solution. Similarly, the editorial on the "secret brotherhood/sisterhood" of countercultural spirituality from *Gnosis* was such an ideological declaration: the contradiction or strain in question concerned the high level of self-autonomy in alternative spirituality that made large-scale affiliation to any one organization highly unlikely, but which collective role enactments thereof still suggested this "brotherhood/sisterhood."

At the same time, as per Sutton and others (see Gieryn 1983:782), ideological claims provide the speaker with a means to promote one's personal *interest*: "They are manipulations of ideas to persuade people to think and act in ways benefiting the ideologist." Again, turning to the issue of self-initiation or the secret brotherhood/sisterhood, it could be argued that these authors not only were addressing the strains or contradictions of this diverse community, but also were promoting this community of whom the authors consider themselves to be a part. Not simply conveying technical information, these articles were serving the interests of the authors, who hoped to persuade the reader of the importance of self-initiation, the secret brotherhood/sisterhood, and/or the overriding alternative spiritual perspective thereof.

Given that these types of statements seem to present and reckon with a contradictory strain while simultaneously promoting the symbolic solution at hand, such assertions could be said to be examples of symbolic capital (Bourdieu 1984, 1994). If "capital" can be viewed as information resources in the form of communication style or social ritual that provide or reinforce social unity, then ways of communicating about countercultural spirituality potentially could be a type of information capital. This information capital can become a form of symbolic capital when (as with economic, or other forms of capital) "it is perceived by social agents endowed with categories of perception which cause them to know it and to recognize it, to give it value" (Bourdieu 1994:8). Those who are able to perceive the symbolic "value" of this capital are those enough enmeshed in the social order to do so, and act as agents of its propagation. Therefore, when alternative spiritualists make ideological declarations concerning the strain and alleged resolution of the paradox of self-autonomy versus community, they are engaging in a recognized form of discourse that symbolically demonstrates one's commitment to countercultural spirituality while also conveying its message to others.

To explore how this ideological and symbolic information helps to build or reaffirm this "secret" community, it is useful to explore scholarship on contemporary social movements.

First, Gusfield (1981, 1994:62; see also Neitz 1994) discusses recent social movements in terms of forces geared at changing meanings more than rigorously associating as a collective. Such groups are relatively unbounded, yet still manage to "manifest a shared direction, a set of goals, and a shared conception of what is right and just as well as a procedure to obtain such goals." Gusfield lists some of the more diffuse aspects of feminism and gay rights, or the hippie movement, as examples of what he calls *fluid social movements*, offering an alternative set of values, explanations or lifestyle choices that are likelier to be enacted in small-scale, everyday — and less public — settings than in traditional, highly organized social movements. However fluid or diffuse such movements are, they — and their participants — nonetheless are identifiable, and suggest some recognizable form of dissension with the existing social order.

One could argue that countercultural spirituality meets the criteria of a fluid social movement. While weak in the way of formal organization or legal/political agendas, it nonetheless promotes an alternative set of values or lifestyle options — such as engaging in spiritual activities with a minimum of dogma or hierarchy, and pronouncing so doing as acts of dissension. However loosely structured this social movement is, certainly those who identity with it often are identifiable (i.e., "New Agers," and so forth) for their flight away from mainstream social controls. Therefore, an emphasis on self-autonomy does not preclude a sense of social solidarity, or an active promotion of shared interests.

Melucci (1985, 1989, 1994; see also Buechler 1995) similarly sees new social movements as existing in symbolic, communicative codes of opposition (often of a spiritual or personalized nature) to the rational pragmatism and control mechanisms of modern society. Not unlike the concept of symbolic capital, these symbolic codes are viewed as deeply embedded in these personalized communication acts that virtually "invisibly" reflect underlying social expectations. Hence, such movements provide participants with identity claims suggestive of social solidarity while also emphasizing an absence of social control that promotes individuality and tolerance for new information. By not being overtly political or class-based, such movements are not easily co-opted by the mainstream power-holders, and so become a stronger collective voice of repudiation against rational society:

> Conflicts do not chiefly express themselves through action designed to achieve outcomes in the political system. Rather, they raise a challenge that recasts the language and cultural codes that organize information. . . . The forms of power now emerging in contemporary societies are grounded in an ability to "inform" that is, to "give form." The action

of movements occupies the same terrain and is in itself a message broadcast to society conveying symbolic forms and relational patterns that cast light on "the dark side of the moon"— a system of meanings that runs counter to the sense that the apparatuses seek to impose on individual and collective events. This type of action affects institutions because it selects new elites, it modernizes organizational forms, and creates new goals and new languages. (Melucci 1994:102)

Melucci's conception, like Gusfield's, suggests that the countercultural spiritual community, by engaging in anti-dogmatic discourse and practices, is opposing what is perceived to be the overly rationalized mainstream society, and it does so through personalized competing claims (sometimes of a spiritual nature) that could be called symbolic codes. Once again, ideological statements concerning the strain between self-autonomy versus community can be viewed as having deeply embedded meanings for the speaker. Furthermore, the alternative spiritual identity suggests both individual needs as well as social ones, whereby discourse pertaining to this type of flexible and adaptable social role suggests both self-autonomy and a sense of being part of a large-scale social movement.

As for Melucci's statement regarding "new elites," it is useful to consider that while countercultural spirituality has been disparaged by both mainstream secular rationality (i.e., the legitimized scientific community) as well as mainline religions, the result has been that an alternative spiritual network has flourished apart from the sanctions of these other institutions, creating its own norms and values (Campbell and McIver 1987; Hess 1993). It has its own language, goals, (albeit fluid) sense of organization, and perhaps even its own elites, if one were to consider ideological discourse made by countercultural spiritualists in terms of symbolic codes or capital. That is, information with certain symbolic meanings promotes the speaker as one who understands the "true" message of alternative spirituality, and so merits being taken seriously as a countercultural spiritualist.

This highly personalized yet socially located ideology finds alternative spiritualists spending considerable time articulating their beliefs and experiences to others; their engagement in spiritual values is not confined to magazines or group events. And so it was of interest to see how people would discuss their spirituality one-on-one, in an interview situation. I wanted to see if comments concerning self-autonomy and community were present, and if so, if there would be similarities across interviewees, suggesting a fluid, modern social movement expressing itself through ideological, symbolic codes or capital.

INTERVIEWING AND ANALYSIS

Interviewing

Just as my theoretical exploration of the countercultural spirituality suggested affinity with numerous sources, so did I utilize numerous strategies in my methodological procedure. As I was interested in seeing what–if any–declarations made in interviews suggested shared ideology, it was useful to analyze these interviews as instances of narrative. Such an analysis assumes that the self largely is a social construct, whereby narratives about the self are a primary means by which social actors utilize and reflect the large-scale norms, values, beliefs and ideologies that they encounter. Hence, narratives are not mere retelling of events, but are the means by which life experience takes on meaning and social value (Mishler 1986; Bennett 1986; Denzin 1989; McCall 1990; Riessman 1993; Calhoun 1994; Somers and Gibson 1994). Therefore, large-scale social forces beyond the self — including ideological allegiances — can be gleaned from narrative accounts.

I utilized Riessman's (1993) approach to narrative analysis for the interviewing process, and enacted a two-step procedure. First, I simply turned on a tape recorder and asked each person to tell me the story of his/her spiritual journey, in as much detail as he/she felt comfortable. I never interrupted a speaker during this phase of the interview, as I did not want to unduly influence the speaker — I wanted to see what shared themes (if any) interviewees brought up themselves, without any prompting from me. Only when the interviewee explicitly stated that he or she was finished with his or her story did I probe for clarification on any of the things he/she had said. This first phase of the interview took anywhere from about twenty minutes to two-and-a-half hours.[6]

In the second phase of the interview, I asked a short, set list of questions to each person. Answers to these questions will be referred to throughout the book. Comparisons across interviewees therefore could be made from open-ended narratives, or from responses to specific items.

While being interviewed, some individuals assumed I must have already known a great deal about countercultural spirituality, and so made little effort to explain what they meant by certain concepts. Other people were constantly saying to me things like, "Do you know what yoga is?" or "Are you familiar with reincarnation?" My response was to say as little as possible, so as not to interrupt the narrative flow. Characteristically, I would say, "Tell me what it means to you," as I tried to assume as little as possible what a given interviewee meant by the things he or she said. When people did not explain what they meant by yoga or reincarnation, I later would ask them what they meant.

I contacted these individuals one year after interviewing them, sharing what I thought to be the main points that emerged both from the specific interview with that person, as well as the similarities that seemed to emerge across interviewees and which would appear to be reflective of alternative spiritual ideology at large. Through doing so, I hoped to increase both the internal and external validity of my eventual claims. When several persons expressed that I was slightly inaccurate in some of my conclusions, I adjusted my ideas accordingly. I also asked the interviewees if they felt that the things they said a year ago reflected their beliefs as of now. Not a single interviewee stated that he or she had dramatically altered his or her beliefs from the year before, though sixteen of them said that their commitment to and understanding of these beliefs had deepened considerably. In about a third of the cases, people also said that while they still believed in basically the same things, they were learning to incorporate more kinds of information into their spirituality.

Analysis

In transcribing upwards of 300 pages of interviews (and in listening to them repeatedly), I began to notice certain kinds of comments being made by all or at least most of the interviewees. This in and of itself was a finding: for all the eclectic and individualized assortments of spiritual beliefs (i.e., self-autonomy), there were certain overriding shared ways of speaking amongst these people suggesting shared symbolic codes or capital, as well as the presence of a fluid social movement.

Denzin (1989:43) discusses *self stories* as one form of narrative. The self is very much the protagonist of such accounts; however, it is a self in relation to a particular context or framework of experiences. Often, self stories reflect the influence of a given social group or role that the speaker is enmeshed in; indeed, they often are told within the explicit confines of a group setting. A self story is spontaneous, "made up as it is told. It does not exist as a story independent of its telling; although, after it has been told, it can take on the status of a story that can be retold."

These interviews literally did not involve the explicit kind of group setting discussed by Denzin. However, given that I was searching for ideology and symbolic capital that reflected one's identity and sense of belonging as a countercultural spiritualist, the concept of "self stories" would seem a useful heuristic for conceptualizing the interviews. Persons discussed their life experience, but within a framework of being an alternative spiritualist, whereby the collective values or ideology of this particular social role could potentially be reflected.

Self stories are relatively spontaneous, reflecting the speaker's sense of social values and normative expectations in a particular moment in time (Denzin 1989). Thus, another might be tempted to label the speaker's assertions as inaccurate, stilted or illusory. However, "[t]he point to make is not whether biographical coherence is an illusion or a reality. Rather, what must be established is how individuals give coherence to their lives when they write or talk self-autobiographies. The source of this coherence, the narratives that lie behind them, and *the larger ideologies that structure them* [my italics] must be uncovered" (Denzin 1989:62).

As ideology underlies self stories, an additional useful heuristic for analysis came from Volosinov's (1973) Marxian analysis of discourse. Volosinov describes the verbal as "the most sensitive index of social changes," and says that it "has the capacity to register all the transitory, delicate, momentary phases of social change" (Volosinov 1973:19). Therefore, states Volosinov, when an individual is articulating his or her beliefs or experiences, he or she simultaneously is referring to information and ideology located outside the self. And so the assertion of one's viewpoint will at very least implicitly — and often explicitly — contain elements of social protest against a majority or domineering ideology that one is reacting against. Hence, it is possible to use this Marxist perspective to see how elaboration of one's countercultural spiritual self story reflects elements not only of a shared alternative spiritual ideology per se but also a reaction *against* a more conventional approach to organization or religion. Such an analysis suggest parallels with Gusfield's and Melucci's discussion of modern, loosely structured social movements, and the ways that a shared, communal protest against mainstream rigidity can be symbolically inferred from personalized yet codified ideological declarations.

Finally, given the element of the supernatural that appeared in the interviews, it was useful to address the issue of narrative coherence. "Coherence" does not necessarily mean true or false, or even credible versus fantastic, but that given the overriding system of belief to explain the events, what happens first, next and last would seem logical and consistent (Mishler 1986; Griffin 1990; Riessman 1990, 1993; Rosenwald and Ochberg 1992; Linde 1993). For example, audiences may not have trouble accepting that a movie hero has supernatural powers, but they might stop suspending disbelief if he says or does something out of character, given these powers. The narrative would cease to be coherent. Similarly, if someone says, "God talks to me every day," and proceeds to tell a story that is consistent with this claim, the speaker has achieved narrative coherence. Such accounts can be deemed *trustworthy*, indicative of deeply enmeshed social patterns that can be located and analyzed, even as they are not necessarily "true" or "false" (Young 1987).

Other Considerations

My analysis herein is limited by space. Also, there was an ongoing quandary between wanting to include an especially interesting passage, versus striving to refer to each interviewee more or less equally in the course of the book. Additionally, while interviewees frequently made comments that suggested similar themes, in some instances they did so more succinctly or vividly than others. Ultimately, I self-imposed an heuristic to refer to a given interviewee a maximum of twice in a given chapter. Hence, any number of excellent passages for analysis unfortunately were excluded.

Furthermore, some passages were so sociologically rich that while I used them to illustrate a particular type of remark, it was possible to use them to illustrate other kinds of remarks as well. Perhaps I was analyzing instances of people discussing alternative spirituality and science, but the passage being quoted also suggested an example of how alternative spiritualists viewed environmentalism, or tried not to be dogmatic. However, I refrained from using the same excerpt more than once.

NOTES

1. To further illustrate the inclusiveness that is attempted, readers were asked to identify their sex as female, male, transsexual male to female, or transsexual female to male. Sexual orientation was classified as heterosexual, bisexual, gay male, lesbian, or celibate. When asked about the "dwelling" they lived in, readers could select among the following: house, apartment, condominium, RV/trailer/bus, room, and prison cell.

2. See Appendix A for a detailed discussion of these different spiritual labels.

3. Over 18 months, I attended events across a three-state region, and acquired numerous informants in the course of doing fieldwork. However, convenience compelled me to interview people who resided in the same region (though a few interviewees were visiting from other parts of the country).

4. All interviewees are referred to by pseudonyms. All told, five people interviewed had returned to college. Obviously, returning students can be found in all walks of life. Still, perhaps this relatively common trend among interviewees suggests a lifestyle in which the individual does not feel especially constrained about seeking new information and/or social possibilities.

5. A substantial number of interviewees were raised Catholic, a fact that future research might wish to pursue in more detail. However, here it should be pointed out that my sample size and qualitative emphasis make me reluctant to assert hasty generalizations concerning alternative spirituality and Catholic childhoods. Also, some of the interviewees were raised in Protestant traditions — or in no religious tradition at all.

6. See Appendix B for a full listing of these questions.

2

Talking about Self-Autonomy and Community

From transcribing and listening repeatedly to the taped interviews, I noticed that not only were there plentiful comments suggesting an ideological strain between self-autonomy and community, but that there were common ways of framing these remarks that suggested the presence of symbolic capital. People who allegedly shunned strong organizational dogma and control nonetheless discussed similar key issues or made similar word choices within the context of their life story. This indicated that these issues and ways of discussing them were deeply enmeshed in the process of becoming an alternative spiritualist, and were in effect tools for discussing alternative spirituality. In this way, it could be argued that collectively the interviewees suggested the presence of a contemporary social movement geared less at overt political action or explicit organization than with protesting and altering established social controls and meanings through interaction and new ways of communicating. By discussing alternative spiritual ideology, the speaker simultaneously was promoting it as symbolically apart from and/or superior to competing claims from mainstream institutions.

EMPHASIS ON SELF

Opening Remarks

Each interviewee's self story was indeed a *self* story, one that very much began, continued and ended with the self. The people I interviewed voiced concern over numerous social issues, and a number of them were involved in volunteer activities. Yet even when people had significant others, they were seldom mentioned (though five people mentioned their children). Going strictly by what was on tape, the listener often would not know if the speaker was single or attached, had ever had children, or if he or she grew up with siblings. One's spiritual experiences and understandings were not assumed to involve anyone but the self. Phrases to the effect of "I suppose I felt like many other people," or "Like anyone else, this was what I wanted," appeared only in one interview.

This rigorous emphasis upon the self was apparent from the opening remarks of each interviewee. People began by discussing their quest for spiritual understanding in a context of conflict with mainstream society and/or the mainline religion of their family of origin. In this way, interviewees began to frame their stories within an ideological context of strain between competing worldviews — and in so doing simultaneously and symbolically promoting the countercultural spiritual perspective. However, the spirituality being sought did not involve a desire to please God, or learn from a figurehead — rather, it was to develop more understanding of the self. Self-knowledge was viewed as spiritual knowledge. Self-autonomy was strongly suggested by these comments. But at the same time, there often was indication of an anomic sense of wanting to connect with others, though being unable for not yet having found alternative spirituality.

Given that interviewees were free to begin the telling of their spiritual journey however they wanted, it is interesting to note that opening remarks fell into three general categories: a feeling of being born "different," a childhood moral/ religious conflict, or an assertion of having always been spiritually empowered. These shared ways of beginning one's story served to heighten the ideological contrast between being part of the mainstream and part of the alternative spiritual movement, and so could be seen as forms of symbolic capital. (The one exception to any of these categories was Arthur, who began by talking about something he had recently been doing.)

Born "Different"

Five interviewees began by stating they felt they were born "different" from other people to a supernatural extent. This "difference" portended to a deeper spiritual consciousness within the self that other people were too enmeshed in the limitations of mainstream society to notice. Thus, the speaker talked of having suffered for feeling out of place in human society. Countercultural spirituality was viewed as the means by which one could develop one's unique self. By so doing, one could start to feel more integrated with the life experience, for one had found a means to express and develop one's true and profoundly spiritual self.

Maria began her story like this[1]:

In hindsight now, I couldn't remember it at the time, but when I — I'd like to go back to my early memories as — I've been digressed back even to my birth. And I think that this a probably a big indi — this is a big part of my spiritual journey because it's a big part of my story is that I was a very difficult birth. My mom had a very traumatic time in my birth, and when I was hypnotically brought back to my birth, um — I didn't want to come out. In fact, the doctor said, "This is a very stubborn baby." And I remember — I mean, these are things that I didn't really remember when I was being hypnotized, but I remember the first thing I said when she brought me back to that moment was, "No, I changed my mind, I'm not going. No, I can wait, I don't want to be on that planet, there's just no way." And, um, it was like the beginning of my rebellion towards ever being here, my — my loneliness towards being here, um, just feeling like an outsider — like, "Who are these people?" I — they're not from my planet, I'm not from this planet, or whatever. Just real isolation kinds of feelings and being an outsider. And I think that, um, you know, I had early kinds of things in my life that probably could have been real mystical, but because of my emotional state of mind, they weren't.

Maria made apparent the strain she felt between deeper spiritual levels of awareness and these other people who were "not from my planet." In so doing, her symbolic point of comparison was spirituality. Because she was so caught up in this foreign way of living, she could not appreciate the "mystical" things happening around her. The story that subsequently unfolded concerned how Maria learned to develop the spiritual potential she was born with by finding sources of information that were more from her "planet" (i.e., the alternative spiritual movement), and how she felt she became a more well-adjusted person for doing so.

Moral/Religious Conflict

Eight of the persons I interviewed began their stories by describing a sense of isolation by perceiving at an early age some form of social contradiction within a mainline religious body[2] These individuals did not talk about feeling like they were from otherworldly realms. They depicted themselves as ordinary people who were seeking basic human decency or understanding from their religions, but felt they were not getting it. The emerging self story was of a protagonist veritably alone against the status quo. Ultimately, each was seeking the answers to be found in countercultural spirituality to resolve the conflict. Thus, these were not viewed as moral conflicts of a fundamentally secular nature, but rather as serving to set in motion the discovery of one's "true" self. After encountering the alternative spiritual movement, one began to develop an increasingly satisfactory outlook on life, though never forgetting the early conflict that a mainline religion could not resolve. In these instances of narrative, the dislike for mainstream worldviews (as enacted by mainline religions) often was extremely pronounced, functioning as a form of symbolic capital insofar as locating the self as a countercultural spiritualist communicating protest toward these religions.

The following scenario was described by Anthony:

I guess originally I was about, uh, eleven or twelve years old that my parents were divorced. Yet my mother's first husband was a drummer who played on showboats going out on the river, and, uh, he was a junkie, so the marriage failed because of drugs, and my mother married a — um, my father. Uh, I was Roman Catholic at the time. That would mean that as a Roman Catholic I would have to hold the belief that my parents were going to, um, suffer eternally for their actions, and it occurred to me that any God or per — or force that would, um, would do this to existent beings would — was more demonic, was more of a demon than — than a God in itself. I think that, plus, um, some early dreams that I had.

From here, Anthony went on at length to describe dreams he had as a child that he felt indicated his destiny to pursue alternative spirituality, symbolically linking the moral issue of the divorce to the mystical. In the course of so doing, he mentioned having a brother, but he did not discuss whether the brother also suffered conflicts over the divorce — or for that matter, if the brother also had significant dreams. The symbolic strain between what was "God" versus what was unforgivingly "demonic" was Anthony's conflict alone. To his viewpoint, it was obvious his mother had made the correct moral choice by divorcing a junkie, and only people overly enmeshed in dogma and social control would believe differently.

Spiritually Empowered

Eight people began by discussing a feeling of always having been spiritually empowered, and therefore logically proceeding to seek out spiritual information. These people did not state they were from another life form, nor that they developed this spiritual viewpoint over a conflict. They matter-of-factly depicted themselves as always having been highly spiritual. These persons, too, seemed to feel at odds with mainstream society and expressed a sense of pleasure in finding people who better understood them. But they did not emphasize feelings of loneliness or struggle. The desire for spiritual information was viewed as outweighing what other people thought of them. Conflicts with mainstream bodies of knowledge had more to do with impatience on the part of the speaker than emotional wounds. For example, Steven began his account in the following manner:

I suppose that it basically began, oh, when I was a kid. I was always interested in mythology, science fiction, fantasy — uh, the more elaborate and detailed, the better. Anyway, and of course I was always interested in magic. My favorite comic book was "Dr. Strange," and I have almost a complete collection. But anyway, I think I was about 16 or so in high school when I finally decided that I must be a Pagan. Mind you — I have never heard of anyone else of that persuasion. At this point, I knew nothing whatever about, uh, Wicca, magic, or any of that. Um, the few books I'd been able to get a hold of in the library's occult section were either like ghost stories or para-psychology, which

I really didn't pay a whole lot of attention to. Or, um, these sort of, um, let's see — "it's all evil and devil worship" kind. I didn't buy that. Anyway, I was only able to get a couple of books on serious magic before I came down to [a] university.

While Steven didn't "buy" into the notion of Paganism being "evil," he did not express encountering any hardship for arriving at this conclusion — he simply knew what he believed, even though no one else in his environment believed similarly. He gave no indication of being challenged beyond what he was capable of understanding — in fact, "the more elaborate and detailed" the information, "the better." Still, Steven expressed a symbolic ideological strain between his essential Pagan nature and what little the mainstream world had to offer insofar as enabling him to enhance it. The rest of Steven's interview reflected this quality of self-assurance. He made no apologies for his outspoken beliefs. Even when he related having experienced a long period of health problems he gave no indication of having suffered second thoughts about his spirituality. In fact, Steven said that his spirituality was what got him thorough this challenging phase, and if anything he emerged more committed than before.

Self as Authority

The contemporary religious experience often sees the self as the final authority as to what to believe or practice, and individuals feel relatively free to pick and choose information from a variety of religious traditions. As both popular literature and spiritual activities would suggest, countercultural spirituality is a highly salient example of this self-autonomy. This was reflected repeatedly in my interviews. Each interviewee was asked to name his or her sources of spiritual information, and each person mentioned the self as the primary source of such information. By so doing, individuals also elaborated on how or why this ideological tenet was featured in alternative spirituality, and less likely to be found in mainstream society by comparison. Locating the self as final authority of one's spirituality became a form of symbolic code or capital insofar as promoting countercultural spirituality, and protesting rigid social control. At the same time self-autonomy was conceptualized as existing in a state of strain with the need forshared values and understanding with others. For example, Sylvia replied as follows when asked to name her sources of spiritual information:

Myself — almost entirely myself. I read books, but generally they don't teach me anything. Um, the inner voice is my best teacher. Um, the world and all my ancestors, I would say, is the second best teacher. Um, most of it is internal. Uh, it varies from one of the — uh, at the early stages that was one of my problems because the everybody [sic] "I am — I am the student of — the student of So-and-So, or I am — this is my tradition, and I am — " You know, all that — I didn't have any of that. Um, for a long time it would bother me, and I kept looking for a source for my spiritual teachings, and finally realized that I wasn't supposed to do that. That I was supposed to do that — that I was supposed to do it on my own, so that everybody could see that they could do it on their own. My whole basis is a phrase that a lot of people have used over and over again which is "everyone is a star," and I take that very literally.

Sylvia addressed a strain she experienced between self-autonomy and the expectation that she find a more rigid, organized process to follow in her quest for spiritual understanding. Ultimately, she grew critical of dogma, yet she also came to believe that "everyone is a star," and so promoted her belief that not only she herself but everyone must find his/her own personalized approach to spirituality. Indeed, by maintaining this self-autonomy she felt she was setting a good example, so that others could "see that they could do it on their own." In these ways, a strain between self and the need for ties with others was addressed. Similarly, Jesse replied as follows to the same question:

Gnosis, direct knowledge. Uh, books can give you hints and directions to where you might look, but you gotta do it. Even if you practice ceremonial magic, it does nothing for me to take a ritual out of a book and perform it. That's just a performance. But if I understand wha-what this ritual is aiming for and how the symbols may help evoke [understanding]. . . . A direct gnosis, or a direct working knowledge of rather than basing it on belief — because some- body told you this and now you must just believe this. I have a hard time believing anything without some form of personal proof, it — now it doesn't have to be objective, it can be subjective, for me, but if I've experienced it, then to me, it — it — I can accept it as true, but if I don't experience it, I can't — I have a very hard time accepting it. I have to check it out myself.

Not unlike Sylvia, Jesse dealt with a strain between personalized spiritual understanding based upon one's own experiences and observations, versus information others might impose upon the self. Again like Sylvia, Jesse believed strongly in self-autonomy in this regard, and promoted this viewpoint accordingly. Symbolic use of language such as "gnosis" was employed to strengthen his claim. Still again like Sylvia, Jesse was part of a growing social network that emphasized firsthand knowledge, not believing something "because somebody told you" to do so.

Self-Autonomy as Spiritual Ideology

Not only did interviewees explicitly state that the self was the primary source of spiritual information, but each interview also contained comments concerning self-autonomy at numerous other points, suggesting that this con- cept had saturated each speaker's alternative spiritual worldview. Such ways of talking seemed to invoke symbolic meaning, promoting countercultural spiri- tuality as differing from mainstream society for the alleged absence of limiting structure or dogma in the former.

Arthur was asked to list his spiritual tools, and replied as follows:

Tarot. My temple [an altar in his home]. Uh, the [study group he facili-
tates]. Uh, a — a sensitivity to people that tries as much as possible to affirm
their — their ability to maintain their own belief system while still questioning
it. I have this [saying] that, that goes, uh, "Believe absolutely everything that
you hear, while simultaneous — simultaneously believing absolutely nothing."
You know, allow yourself to create your own belief systems.

The question did not require that Arthur promote his agenda regarding
self-autonomy, but he found an opportunity to do so nonetheless. He included
his "sensitivity" to diversity as a symbolic form of spiritual tool. Though spirituality was seen in terms of self-autonomy, to do so (according to Arthur)
required a social arena of mutual respect. Useful information could be acquired
from outside sources, but ultimately it was up to the self to decide — as indicated by the seeming paradoxical strain of his favorite saying. Arthur asserted it
was possible to both respect and to question, and in reckoning with this strain
he asserted the overriding ideology of the countercultural spiritual movement
as a means of doing so.

Melanie was asked what it meant to say that someone was "on the path,"
and this was her answer:

Being on the path, to me, means getting those things to a place so you can
help others and help yourself and in return, um, [to] grow and grow beyond,
um, the physical and move on either to your next reincarnation, where you
learn the next lesson that you need to learn or move on from this plane. But the
path is helping other people to get on theirs as well. Um, just, um, staying out
of people's way when they don't want help. It's — it's like intuition, kind of.
You — you do it and you feel — if you feel you should help someone or not.
I'm not explaining it very well — it's kind of like . . . not listening to, um, conformity in the masses and what people think society is, but being able to say, "I
am an individual and this is what I believe." Even in the heart of — I don't want
to say "the enemy," but someone who has very different beliefs, and, uh, everybody has different paths. They're not necessarily peaceful, you know, but to me
— mine hopefully is sometimes — not lately, but, um, basically, you know —
mine is just to be a good, uh, person and learn and help others to grow as well
as myself.

Melanie discussed a strain between being attentive to the needs of others
and knowing when to leave them alone in terms of being "on the path,"
whereby the strain took on symbolic significance beyond the arena of mere
social norms. She further conceptualized it as relevant to "the masses," addressing even the issue of their being an "enemy" of spirituality — though she also
stated that there is no real enemy because each person simply follows a "differ-

ent path." In elaborating on these various strains, Melanie promoted self-autonomy through nonconformity as expressed in alternative spirituality.

Resistance to Labels

That the countercultural spiritualist is ideologically opposed to rigid organizational structure was evidenced by another type of remark commonly heard in interviews. Though all twenty-two of the interviewees spent a great deal of their discretionary time and money on their spiritual pursuits, twenty of them explicitly avoided labeling their beliefs or practices. (And the two exceptions suggest special cases, which will be discussed later.) Characteristically, interviewees would list certain traditions as being important to them, only to interject a disclaimer that he/she was not, however, "officially" a part of this tradition. This was one of the ways that the ideological tension between self autonomy and community was addressed. Such remarks took on a symbolic importance, and were one of the ways one identified the self as being an alternative spiritualist, as well as promoted the agenda thereof as being superior to rigid structure.

For example, in the following excerpt, Jerry described a significant spiritual event he attended as follows:

I went to this festival called [name], at that time it was still being held in [state], and it was really good for me, because I saw all these other people that I could relate to spiritually. And they were not Christians, but they were not these terrible people that I was told they would be. And from there, it [his spirituality] really accelerated. It was considered a Pagan gathering, but I don't necessarily consider myself a Pagan. But I don't say that I'm not one, either. Um, it was good because it was a realization that there's something beyond what I was being taught, because I — I believed in the basic principles of Christianity. You know, to love yourself and to love your God and to love — love the people around you. But I couldn't deal with the politics that go with that, too. And now, I can have my — my own religion, which really is a religion based on many different spiritual paths of, uh — like shamanism and some Wicca, and some — very eclectic from different backgrounds and — and a pretty good brew of just things that I've learned, so it's one of my own making.

Jerry addressed ideological strain between group homogeneity versus self-autonomy. He elaborated on the strain itself while also offering a symbolic reckoning with it by being ambiguous as to whether or not he called himself a "Pagan." At the same time, Jerry promoted his approach to this strain as highly workable — he was able to avoid "the politics" that go with more organized religious expressions. Moreover, he made it clear that he felt that this personalized spirituality existed apart from the Christianity he was taught, and which ultimately he did not prefer. Thus, in stating that he is/is not a Pagan, Jerry was expressing a form of paramount symbolic capital within countercultural spirituality, managing to promote alternative spirituality, and criticizing mainline Christianity in the process.

Gypsy also talked about a group event as being significant in her spiritual development, and went on to describe her spirituality as follows:

I do follow by a lot of different spiritual paths. I don't consider myself — I call myself a witch but I'm not Wiccan. I study tantric techniques, but I'm not a tantric Buddhist. Uh, I do dream work techniques, but I don't really follow that original path. Um, I look into Native American studies and at what they have, but I don't consider that my path. I'm very eclectic — I like this idea of pulling from all different sources to find what works for me . . . diversity is the key. Whatever works for you is great as long as you don't hurt anybody else. I think it's fair. It's about the only creed that I expect everyone to follow — don't fuck with anybody else's business, you know. That's why I have a problem with a lot of the mainstream religions, because they're fucking with other people's business.

Similarly to Jerry, Gypsy found that she learned at a festival to develop a highly personalized form of spirituality that emphasized self-autonomy *and* group cooperation. In dealing with this strain — and in promoting the countercultural spiritual solution in the process — Gypsy also criticized more organized religions that would, in her view, attempt to be more dogmatic or rigid. She gave indication of this alternative spiritual worldview being both personalized and shared with others, whereby her disclaimers regarding the labeling of her spirituality could be seen as a form of symbolic capital.

As mentioned earlier, two interviewees (Jack and Steven) technically did label their spiritual beliefs. But these self-imposed "labels" hardly revealed a strong endorsement of dogma. For example, consider this passage from Jack as he described his disenchantment with the Catholicism of his childhood, and his incipient interest in countercultural spirituality:

I turned to reincarnation instead, and found that it was a better answer to the, uh, the problems in this world. You know, like some people are born blind, or some people are born poor. I think reincarnation is the better answer. So I stuck with that, and, uh, I kind of grew away from Catholicism [and] I read a book by, uh, Marion Zimmer Bradley called *Mists of Avalon*, which talks about, uh, King Arthur and Merlin and all that, and she talks about the Goddess in there. And that's another option that I decided to take into my religion — uh, referring to God not as a "God," but as a "Goddess," and so I kind of started leaning toward Wicca religion and all that kind of stuff. I'm not a practicing witch or anything. I just — I'm in the — in the, uh, rituals they do and all that. And, um, I'm interested in all the Pagan rituals which they have also. And so I started experimenting with that also, with Wicca and, uh, the Goddess. That kind of stuff. So basically, I — I don't go to church anymore. I've taken up a new [Hindu] meditation, and that's what I do as part of my religion — mediate everyday, twice a day, uh, when — if I — if I can have the time for it. And so my religion basis — it's of more Hindu religion now and Wiccan religion together. So, um, I do believe in a lot of Hindu thoughts. I have a lot of Hindu books. Um, I've taken two Hindu classes. So I know a little about Hindu religion, and uh, I guess my religion would be more Hindu than Catholic right now, so — basically, I'd probably count myself a Hindu religion guy right now. And that's basically where I'm at right now — reincarnation and the Goddess and that kind of stuff.

Technically, Jack labeled himself "a Hindu religion guy" — albeit only for "right now." But given the eclectic assortment of information that accompanied this identity, Jack ultimately also was expressing a highly individualized approach to spirituality in which new forms of information were welcomed and not rejected. There was little if any rigidity and considerable self-autonomy in Jack's belief system. (He even made a disclaimer regarding his being "not a practicing witch or anything.") This spiritual approach was discussed within the context of flight away from the Catholicism of Jack's childhood, whereby he reckoned with a symbolic strain between competing systems, coming out on the side that offered him the opportunity to personalize his beliefs.

Steven was the one person I interviewed who belonged to a relatively organized spiritual group, and who explicitly labeled himself Neo-Pagan. However, he also stated:

In practical terms, of course, I can work with a lot of people, even if we're not theologically in sync, as one of the things about Paganism is that practice is more important than doctrine. With no central authority, how can there be [a] universally accepted doctrine? Christianity doesn't — doesn't have that. Islam doesn't have that, for that matter. No religion really has it, and it seems to be axiomatic that only a handful, maybe five percent of practitioners of a certain religion have any real idea what the religion is actually about, and quite often these people are not the official leaders at all.

While Steven technically labeled himself a Pagan, he freely admitted to working with persons who were not necessarily Pagans but who were part of this informal spiritual movement. He promoted the concept of the absence of "central authority" as a means of explanation, and critiqued more organized religions in the process. While Steven noted that these other bodies also do not have a "universally accepted doctrine," he still managed to be critical of these groups, in that the persons who truly practiced other doctrines often "are not the official leaders." Presumably, some people had a more internalized, personalized understanding. Steven mitigated with symbolic strains between official doctrine and how the self might actually practice spirituality, and promoted his countercultural viewpoint in the process.

General Yet Personalized

In alternative spirituality, information is offered through literature and group activities, whereby there is *some* shared understanding about a given practice or belief system. Yet there remains an emphasis on each person deciding for him/herself what the belief or practice in question should mean. This strain often is addressed through statements such as "I can only speak for myself," or "Everyone has to find their own way." These types of remarks were heard in twenty-one of the interviews (the one exception being Steven). Such declarations took on a symbolic meaning, in that they were recognizable as group ideology. They were one of the ways that countercultural spiritualists use communication codes to break away from what they see to be the dogma and over-rationalization of the mainstream, and promote their norms and values by contrast.

Alex stated the following in the first few minutes of her interview:

It's hard to like just talk about it [spirituality]. Um, but it's like, you know, when people talk about — everybody, I guess everybody who does it has any — I don't know if you can call it Paganism, or you can call it, you know, whatever you want, I guess, but it's usually — everybody usually has their own individual interpretation of what they talk about, when they say things like "Goddess," or, you know, "Demeter," or something like that. For me, I guess, when I say "Goddess," I mean like it's not really a deity that I speak of, or some, like, woman, you know, up in the sky, or something, it's more like — it's more like an energy.

Disparaging of literalists who would conceptualize a deity in dogmatic terms, Alex instead used socially-located, generalized names and terminologies to discuss a highly-personalized symbolic conceptualization of deities. She simultaneously promoted the alternative spiritual flight away from rigidity in declaring that this spirituality could be called whatever someone wanted to call it. Those who practiced this spirituality "everybody who does it" were depicted as understanding the deeply-enmeshed symbolic implications of these ideas. In dealing with the strain between the general and the personalized, Alex promoted her countercultural spiritual agenda while also being careful to state that her opinions were only what worked for her.

Somewhat similarly, Flora described her spiritual activities as follows:

One thing that I do on an almost daily basis is that I greet my guardian spirit. I greet that part of myself that's not in the three-dimensional universe. Um, some people call it their guardian spirit, some call it your guardian angel, your higher self, your fourth-dimensional double — whatever you call that part of yourself. Um, I greet that part of myself every morning, or every night, and I thank it for being with me, and staying present with me — which is really kinda unnecessary, because it is there whether I like it or not [laughter]. And —

but I do that as a form of honoring, and I ask to be able to be in touch with that part of myself, and to act in the best interest of all beings, and to act in the best interests of myself, and to come from a compassionate place always. That's like my daily prayer. And I greet other people's guardian spirits when I remember. I'm getting better at remembering. It takes a while to remember to do that every time you see people, um, and ask that part of them to be present, and to work with that part of me. And I ask those parts of us to protect us. So that's something I do every day.

Flora stated that there was a spiritual dimension of self likely to be labeled differently by individuals because of their disparate spiritual ideas, yet which also fundamentally signified the same thing. Her communing with this spiritual aspect of self was seen as a symbolic means by which to also connect with other people — to act in her own best interests, as well as the best interests of others. Flora then went on to assert that other people have this same spiritual force guiding them, something both personalized yet common among individuals. Strains between personal goals and the well-being of others were addressed through the alternative spiritual ideology she advanced, in which the honoring of self-autonomy *across individuals* was seen as a means toward creating a more humane world.

Unique Yet Overlapping Belief Systems

One question that proved telling was whether or not the interviewee ever met other people who shared his/her beliefs. All twenty-two of the interviewees answered this question similarly, suggesting a form of symbolic capital. In effect, each person stated that he/she would never meet anyone who absolutely believed the same way, because each person was unique; however, there was a community of persons that reflected a certain common ground or overlap of belief. And this community was viewed as providing a means for sharing with others who fundamentally were fellow travelers despite superficial differences of belief. In this way, interviewees symbolically addressed and reckoned with a strain between self-autonomy and community, while also promoting the countercultural spiritual approach to this strain as highly viable. For example, Badger said:

Sometimes I meet with people that share some of them [his spiritual beliefs]. You know, it's all varied. Uh, I do, I do — uh, really connect with certain people. I haven't met anybody that I could agree with everything on, but I've met with people that will say, "It's okay if you do that over there, just don't pollute where I'm at, and keep it in your space."

For Badger, what mattered was not so much technical agreement but a sense that two people could disagree but still respect each other. Simultaneously, Badger addressed the need for self-autonomy and a sense of shared values with others — people he could "really connect" with. (And there was partial overlap between his beliefs and those of other people, as he met people who "share some of" his beliefs.) Badger discussed a strain between similar and diverse beliefs across individuals while also advancing the alternative spiritual perspective away from strong social control over others.

Iris answered this question as follows:

That's a good question — yes and no. There is no one I'm going to meet who shares exactly the same doctrine or dogma or — or even belief about what, uh, what any given word means. You know, what karma means to you is going to mean something different to me. But yet we can still talk about karma in a — in a similar context. So technically, no, I don't think I'm ever going to run into anybody who believes exactly as I do. I do, however, have a very close community that our beliefs are similar enough that we share ritual, we share, um, spiritual time together. Um, I have a woman's group that I — you know, I feel like I'm — my beliefs are radically different from them, but we meet every month for ritual, and we have, um, [a] very spiritual, very emotionally satisfying experiences.

Again, the interviewee stated that there was partial overlap between her own spiritual beliefs and those of others — Iris viewed her beliefs simultaneously as unique yet shared by others. In discussing this paradoxical strain, she advanced not only the countercultural spiritual ideological emphasis on self-autonomy, but also her positive experience within this community, and the strong solidarity ties she had acquired. Iris's comments took on a dimension of symbolic capital for their underlying representativeness of countercultural spirituality as a whole.

Importance of Alternative Spiritual Community

Each person I interviewed spoke of some sort of event or group experience giving him or her a unique sense of interconnectedness with others while still being able to enact his or her individualized conception of self. Hence, these comments suggested an ideological recognition of the strain between self-autonomy and community, as well as an effort to resolve the strain, whereby the countercultural spiritual movement was promoted.

Eli described his initial encounter with a group of alternative spiritualists as follows:

Uh, at first, I was just attracted to it immediately. People who didn't think I was a geek, as most people did. Uh, they were people who were willing to help me to classify my experiences and my desires, um, my — and my dysfunctions into a cohesive worldview. You know, all of a sudden, "Hey, look, you're not a freak, you're a human being, and this is where you fit into the scheme of humanity, these are the energies you're playing with, this is what's going on, this has meaning."

Eli made apparent how and why he would have preferred associating with countercultural spiritualists rather than with more mainstream persons who found him to be "a geek." Alternative spirituality did not criticize but encouraged qualities that made him feel cut off from mainstream society. At the same time, Eli stated he found a way toward a "cohesive worldview" for the shared norms, values, and beliefs of alternative spirituality. This process further enabled him to feel a part of the overall "scheme of humanity." Thus, countercultural spirituality enabled Eli both to develop his sense of individuality and to feel part of a shared system of meanings — as well as part of humanity at large. The symbolic strain between self-autonomy and the need for community ties was addressed, with Eli's identification with the alternative spiritual movement affirmed in the process.

Ralph described drumming as a "healing" activity. When asked to explain what he meant, he gave the following answer:

It's like you can have all this stuff building up inside you, you know, things that need to come out. Things that — it's like your energy can be shooting all over your body. But when you come together with a bunch of people and become like one energy, you know, like one — say you're playing one heartbeat. . . . It forms a community, you know what I mean? It forms like, uh, like, almost like, you know, a church is like a community. That's the main reason I think why people go to church is because everybody else is there, and to feel this "community-ness" around them together and they're all together, you know, and uh, it heals me in the sense that it puts my life, like — gives it, like, uh — I feel more balanced, more centered, like more I can flow my energy in whatever direction I want, you know what I mean? Lots of different people who are doing it [drumming], it's spreading across the nation in a big way. There's gonna be a big world drumming festival in [a state] for five days long this summer for world peace. I'm gonna be goin' there, and you know, there'll be thousands of people gathered in a huge sky dome drumming for like a week long, and I'm sure that'll be real healing. But, uh, it just — I feel like I connect with — you feel like you connect with people on a different level, like on a spiritual level, and it's like, it doesn't matter, you know, what color, or how they talk, or what they look like, but they can — everyone's got the same heartbeat going . . . and you feel like a oneness with people and it's healing.

Ralph seemed to have found the actual "healing" aspects of drumming to be somewhat ineffable. But he had no trouble communicating approbation for the "community-ness" of such activities. The emphasis simultaneously was on the "energy" within the self and the connections being made to other people who were able to express their individuality in the way of color, speech, and appearance, yet also feel part of this "same heartbeat." He also stated that this was a growing social movement of sorts, and he felt that through such endeavors, goals such as "world peace" could be helped along. For Ralph, the symbolic meaning of drumming seemed to be considerably deeper than the superficial aspects of the act itself. He likened the experience to going to "church," though he did not practice the religion of his family of origin (elsewhere stating that he found it philosophically limited for its many rules, and at times racist). Ralph clearly stated why he was so enthusiastic about countercultural spirituality while dealing with a certain strain between self-healing and community ties with others.

Other Social Opportunities Less Viable

Not only was the alternative spiritual community seen as an important means of manifesting self-autonomy while maintaining strong ties with others, but other possible expressions of community were expressly seen as less viable in accomplishing this. Once again, these comments (which appeared in all twenty-two of the interviewees) suggested that a strain between self-autonomy and community was being addressed, and that the countercultural spiritual agenda was being promoted as a superior means of resolving it. For example, Edward commented at one point:

You see, each of us who are on these kinds of pathways are doing so in isolation, if you will. We are emphasizing that part of our — of the common reality which is unique to us, and through that we are seeing the outer or fundamental part which is behind [it]. Therefore, it boils down to subjective spirituality. There is no single objective pathway that I've found yet that would account for all of the variations.

Edward made the strain between self-autonomy and commonality with others apparent when discussing things like "the common reality which is unique to us." In advancing this countercultural spiritual approach, he flatly stated that more objective, dogmatized belief systems were in his experience unable to "account" for this important expression of individuality. Edward promoted individual approaches to spirituality, yet explained this phenomenon as being part of a larger social trend (i.e., "each of us"), suggesting symbolic meaning beyond the self in his words.

Mary Lou was asked if she faced any challenges to her spirituality in her daily life, and gave the following answer:

There's a daily challenge for me to exclude a part of myself, to respond to people as they want me to be this little box of category that they can easily define and uh, I think that's a challenge for me to say, "I'm whole, I'll always be whole." That's what my — I mean, I'm always — uh, you know, in this multiple kind of faceted form, that, uh, um — and I continue to grow and everything, and when people want to exclude a part of me, to uh, chop off the part that they need, they can only do that with uh my approval, and I'm not willing to do that. Also, just, you know, that goes along with people's, um, uh, racism and sexism. I think those are constant challenges. They sound like political things but I think that from my point of view that's a very spiritual matter.

Mary Lou symbolically conceptualized a strain between social issues such as racism and sexism alongside her strongly-felt need for self-autonomy — all of which was framed within the context of her spirituality. There also was a strain in her life between living up to her own expectations versus the more limiting, rigid expectations of others. But she stated that her spirituality involved a sense of reckoning with this strain in such a way as to give her more confidence to express her full self. Therefore, Mary Lou promoted her spiritual identity, and her everyday efforts to try to be her "whole" self. This process, in her mind, could not be carried out in more traditional kinds of social institutions.

CONCLUSION

Although alternative spiritualists emphasize self-autonomy, there is also a strong sense of shared community values amongst such individuals. That countercultural spiritualists themselves articulated both a sense of self-autonomy and community in talking about themselves suggests not only an awareness of this strain, but also shared symbolic communication codes across individuals. Individually and collectively, attacks were launched against mainstream social controls while promoting alternative spirituality by contrast. Table 2.1 indicates the extensiveness of these ideological similarities.

Table 2.1: Frequencies of Self-Autonomy/ Community Comments in Interviews

Frequencies of Self-Autonomy/ Community Comments in Interviews	N=22	Percent of Sample
Self-Autonomy in Opening Statements	21	95
Self as Authority	22	100
Resistance to Labels	20	91
Self-Autonomy as Spiritual Ideology	22	100

Frequencies of Self-Autonomy/ Community Comments in Interviews	N=22	Percent of Sample
Generalized Yet Personal	21	95
Unique Yet Overlapping Beliefs	22	100
Importance of Alternative Spiritual Community	22	100
Other Social Opportunities Less Viable	22	100

To an extent, my analysis could end at this point. The types of comments addressed offered considerable information as to how alternative spirituality simultaneously could appear to offer both self-autonomy and a shared sense of community. But the ideological common ground across interviewees did not end with explicit talk of self-autonomy or community. There were other overriding ideological concerns that gave further indication of alternative spirituality being an informal social movement, while still affording people the opportunity to emphasize the self.

NOTES

Excerpts from this chapter have been published in a somewhat different form in *Journal for the Scientific Study of Religion* Vol. 37 (No. 2); pgs 288-304 "Individualism and Community in Alternative Spiritual 'Magic'."

1. I quote from interviews verbatim, deleting within segments only when excessive "ums" and "uhs" (or other superfluous utterances) diminish the clarity of the statement. When a segment of copy has been deleted, there is an ellipsis (. . .). Similarly, two segments of transcription might be bridged with a bracketed word, for example "[and]." Brackets also are used to delete words that threaten the interviewee's anonymity. Punctuation has been inserted for intelligibility.

2. "Mainline religion" refers to relatively organized Judeo-Christian denominations that could be characterized as having relatively explicit doctrine — whether liberal, moderate or conservative.

3

Ideological Strains: Spirituality and Science

An important shared belief among alternative spiritualists is that secular rationality has created a false dichotomy between "matter" and "spirit." Mainline religions often are seen as having lost much of their spiritual authenticity by adopting an apologist stance in the presence of this dualistic, secular rationality.[1] By contrast, it is posited that in countercultural spirituality all aspects of life are viewed as sacred. Virtually any life pursuit can be considered an aspect of one's spirituality — case in point, the domain of science. Alternative spiritualists often state that science has been used toward negative ends (pollution, inhumane experiments, and so forth), but the problem has not been with science per se but with the dualistic framework within which it has been enacted. They argue that the laws of science reflect the spiritual interconnections of all aspects of life, and a new form of science can be articulated that advances discourse within a spiritual frame of reference. Countercultural spiritualists believe that theirs is the domain where such articulation is beginning to happen, in contrast to the relatively ineffectual domains of mainstream science and mainline religion (Stone 1978; Adler 1986; Campbell and McIver 1987; Starhawk 1989; Albanese 1992; McGaa 1992; Hess 1993).

There is considerable evidence of this viewpoint in popular literature. For example, a recent issue of *Green Egg: A Journal of the Awakening Earth* (note the title's reference to the *earth,* given that it is a *spiritual* publication) featured Hellenic Paganism (i.e., Greek mythology). One article was entitled "Orpheus in Orbit: Reframing Hellenistic Dualism of the Body and the Earth" (Eyer 1995:5). The author's contention was that ancient Orphic mysteries concerning the soul's ultimate journey apart from the body has been misinterpreted to suggest a false dichotomy:

Two millennia of mind-body dualism have been enough for Western culture. What was a liberating perspective for the Orphic initiates became a rigid dogma under the yoke of Christianity. The church's unchecked abuse of natural resources and relentless denigration of the body and sex have decorated our neurotic refusal to accept ourselves as biological creatures. It seems the legacy of Orphic dualism is humanity's perceived alienation from the natural world . . . what we know, which the Orphic initiates didn't, is that our bodies are constructed by complex proteins called DNA, which contain detailed traces of our evolutionary past and embodying any number of possible options for the future evolution of the species. Without resorting to any kind of supernaturalism, it is possible to derive a positive, ecological and humanistic vision from the still-vibrant lyre of Orpheus.

This ideological argument presents and addresses a symbolic strain between scientific and spiritual forms of understanding, and claims to resolve this strain, promoting the interests of alternative spirituality in the process. That is, elements of what the speaker believes to be science were utilized, but in a manner that fundamentally is aimed at verifying countercultural spirituality, not science as such.

Comments from interviewees dealing with this strain were common enough to suggest the symbolic capital of an informal social movement. Overriding ideological commonalty indicated solidarity and community in the absence of a unified organizational structure, while also promoting the alternative spiritual agenda — and its critique against mainstream society.

RESOLVING DUALISMS

Critical of Mainstream

Before exploring what interviewees said about science, it is helpful to briefly address just how strongly people felt that mainstream social institutions were upholding false dualisms between spirit and matter. Contrastingly, countercultural spirituality was advanced as a means by which one could see past these dualisms and seek to create a holistic worldview. When addressing such dualisms, there often was an element of praxiological social protest. Society, religion (or for that matter, science) were faulted not only on epistemological grounds, but because of some of the very real damage dualistic thinking was alleged to have caused.

Mainstream Society as Dualistic

Each of the twenty-two interviewees gave indication of believing that mainstream society was trapped in dualistic ways of thinking, and so was relatively ineffective insofar as solving global problems. When asked his opinion of mainstream society, Jesse could well have been speaking for all interviewees when he replied as follows:

Very primitive, very trapped in duality and polarization. Uh, very black and white. Has a difficult time seeing shades and colors between things. Um, I see — where I perceive it all as a continuity, it tends to want to divide and separate it, and so it's very kind of like warlike in its nature. And if you looked at the manifestation of that from space, you'd see giant cities called cancer cells across the face of the planet. It scares the piss out of me.

Jesse's criticism of mainstream society being dualistic was straightforward, as well as the way he contrasted it with his alternative spiritual approach. A strain between ways of knowing and dualisms was addressed, while Jesse's personal agenda of seeing the world in terms of "continuity" was promoted at the same time.

Larry voiced a similar sentiment, even though the word "dualism" was not literally used:

I think of it if anything as a virus that's gone a little out of control. Um, uh, somewhere around the industrial revolution, things really kicked in to the point where we can produce the information that is society much more rapidly than we had previously been able to, and, uh, it's gone completely nuts, so it's if anything sorta like a cancer now. Uh, it's a — it's a — an organism that has begun reproducing completely out of control. Uh, and — uh, that — that's my view of mainstream society. Um, does that mean that it's sick, does that mean that it's wrong? Well, no, I don't like making those kind of moral judgments because I don't use that kind of moral system. However, I would like to draw attention to the fact that we are reproducing madly with no real sense of what kind of the [sic] function we're performing, or what it is that we're doing.

Like Jesse, Larry used the metaphor of "cancer" to describe the linear rationality of mainstream society. He not only asserted his view that society was "completely out of control," but went on to depict himself as one who did not make simplistic or dualistic "moral judgments." Larry's ideological declaration addressed the strain between what is functional for the planet and how mainstream society was operating by contrast, and he advanced his personal worldview simultaneously.

Mainline Religions As Dualistic

At some point during each interview, all but one of the interviewees[2] made similar declarations regarding mainline religions as dualistic. Sylvia gave a succinct example of interviewees' sentiments when asked to respond to the word "dualism":

Boring, tedious, limiting. You did say "dualism," didn't you? [I answer affirmatively] Christian. Um, gosh, I hope no Christians are listening to this. Um, I don't mean to be quite this scathing about it, um, I just — dualism and dichotomy is, er — not dichotomy — dualism and, um, dyadic stuff — um, yes or no, um, I have — I have tried to get away from. I have — for a number of years, I have been consistently putting my mindset into thinking about triads, and quatra [levels] to get myself out of, um, that kind of dualistic thing, um, and living more in the gray. It's both [a] psychotherapeutic value as well as a spiritual value.

Sylvia contrasted the limitations of what she believed to be Christian dualistic thinking with her countercultural spiritual worldview that sought to look beyond dualisms to more sophisticated models of interconnectedness. In being able to resolve this strain, she claimed to enhance both her spiritual and psychological sense of well-being — suggesting further interconnectedness between spirituality and other aspects of life.

There were comments that did not literally address religion in terms of dualism but still suggested sympathy with the concept. For example, Ralph was asked to explain what he meant by the word "sacred":

"Sacred" I guess means, uh, part — part of the one. You know, part of God, part of — everything's interconnected and it's all part, you know — it's part of us. The tree's part of us, the grass is part of us and everything, you know, has a meaning, and it should be like the ground, you know, should be like a sacred spot, and treated like, you know — it shouldn't be, you know, like a lot of things are happening, like the water shouldn't be having oil dumped in it. You know, people just — it's like a lot of men, you know, or us men, you know, we don't really care too much about a lot of — don't care, but it's like we gotta make this money, we gotta build this corporation, and whatever's around it can just go to hell, you know. It's like you have to live in unity with what's around you, instead of being so overpowering over it. [My parents] say — well, you know, "What are you doin' out in the woods, why don't you go to church?" You know what I mean? And they don't understand that, you know, that like the earth is like a church. You know, every — the earth is sacred in it's own way.

Ralph discussed "sacred" in terms of interconnections between different aspects of life, whereby things of the earth that one encounters everyday ought to be treated with more reverence. In advancing his beliefs, Ralph also asserted a contrast between what his parents would see as a "church" — a mere edifice — with his holistic, alternative spiritual viewpoint that embraced the entire earth as a church, and therefore sacred. In dealing with dualistic strains between spirit and matter, Ralph promoted countercultural spirituality.

Science as Story

In the first half of each interview, when people talked for as long as they wanted about their spiritual journey however they saw fit, all twenty-two interviewees made reference to science and spirituality in a manner that appeared to be aimed at ideologically resolving any strain between the two knowledge claims. Their comments suggested that alternative spirituality provided ways of reconceptualizing science within a spiritual context.

In fact, in 12 out of the 22 cases, mention of this alleged strain was made in the individual's opening remarks. For example, at the beginning of her account, Marcie related the following:

I grew up in, uh — my mother was uh Irish Protestant, although she acted more like an Irish Catholic, and told me lots of stories about, uh, Irish mythology in particular — the little people, the fairies and elves. And my father, who *was* an Irish Catholic, became a total atheist and scientific method person. Um, he was — he's a [social scientist], and so I had this real polarized view of things at a young age. On one hand, I really loved the fairy tales, the magic, and, uh, questions about God growing up in [time period] in a small rural [name of state] community, where everyone, of course, was, you know, Baptist or something. Like and uh, so and then — and then on the other side, being analytic and uh, questioning belief systems. Um, as I grew older I — I just had this real interest in — in a lot of mythology, in a lot of Celt stuff. And I'm not sure where that comes from unless it's influenced by my mother . . . I read a lot of philosophy as a young teenager, and uh, I just wanted to know, I just wanted to know what I believed in, and why people believed things. And I guess that kind of describes where I'm still — what I'm still doing, um, what is my — what I define as spirituality I'm not quite sure. Somebody asked me that the other night, he's a professor and atheist also, but he found it very curious that most of his friends described themselves as spiritual people, not necessarily religious, but spiritual, and we said, "But you are, too." And I think — I believe he had a narrow definition of what spirituality was.

For Marcie, the ideological strain between science and the spiritual was significant enough to have been symbolically embodied by her parents. She attempted to resolve it through her highly adaptable countercultural spiritual worldview. Admitting to conflict over the more rationalistic side of her nature, Marcie nonetheless asserted herself as fundamentally spiritual. She was critical toward the highly rationalized atheistic professor for having too "narrow" a sense of the spiritual, thereby advancing the alleged all-inclusiveness of the alternative spiritual movement.

Edward also began by talking about science and spirituality:

It started quite a long time ago — when I was around seven, actually. And I had an incredible interest in the world around me, and the best thing that I knew at the time was the sciences. So I studied them in extreme detail, and I also went into lots of other fields. So, um, towards — by the time I was 18, I had a very reasonable broad base of knowledge, and I was branching out into the esoteric philosophies at that point, because nothing quite satisfied my quest for knowledge.

It still doesn't [laughter], but, um, I've got a mixture of creative ability of my — I write things, I build, and I'm a poet, that kind of thing, plus I can do technical — I could — I can design machinery, a lot of people have found that very strange, that those qualities don't fit in the same head, and I didn't really care what others thought. It was what they knew [that mattered], and I've drained all my teachers as dry as I could of knowledge, and went on a kept reading, and I also — by virtue of being somewhat very oriented rationally, if it wasn't describable by equation or measurable, it wasn't a valid phenomenon, or real. At the same time, I felt my perceptions were extremely valuable and real and valid, so when I — I found myself having conscious astral projective experiences, uh, healing experiences, both given and, uh, output — I began to question that, and I found zero evidence for these kinds of things in conventional science, either in quantum theory or relativity. I therefore set out to develop my own [theories].

Not unlike Marcie, Edward experienced a form of strain between scientific and spiritual domains of understanding. He reckoned with it by conceptually subsuming scientific information within an overriding spiritual worldview. Elements of science were utilized to arrive at a spiritual understanding, not the other way around. Ultimately, Edward was somewhat dismissive of the utility of mainstream science, strongly favoring his countercultural spiritual approach. Scientific terminologies functioned as a form of symbolic capital, embedded in a spiritual context that identified the speaker as an eclectic and relatively self-autonomous alternative spiritualist, and potentially lending credence to his claim.

"Correcting" Science

The alleged dualistic tendencies of mainstream science were apparent not only in opening comments made in interviews. In all twenty-two cases, there were indications of the interviewee attempting to point out the limitations of science at various points in his or her account. For example, Steven conveyed the following midway through his opening story:

Basically, with Descartes in the six — seventeenth century on and such, they decided to divide the universe into material, which science can deal with, and non-material, which religion is supposed to deal with. But about the nineteenth century, after science basically won, sci — science declared that the immaterial [sic] didn't exist. Even as scientific research was leading in exactly the opposite direction in many instances. And even though individual scientists and most really good scientists will say that materialism is a bad idea, and it doesn't work, that it does not describe reality, science as a whole tends to follow it.

Steven's disdain for mainstream science was straightforwardly offered as he elaborated on the strain of the alleged false dualism between "material" and "non-material." Scientifically relevant word choices functioned as a form of symbolic capital to identify and advance his countercultural spiritual claim. He also indicated evidence of a trend for science to be enacted more in a way that measured up to the standards of alternative spirituality, i.e., "really good scientists" did not see science as a domain that should address only matter.

Other interviewees elaborated on the strain between science and spirituality in more pragmatic terms. Clarissa observed:

Holistically, people are viewed as more than just their physical bodies. They have a mind and spirit, your emotions, and that's all connected. And what traditional medicine does, you know, like just regular doctors, they just treat the physical symptoms. And every illness, you know, whether it's mental, or, you know, physical, has an emotional root, or a spiritual root. And as long as you ignore that, you're just gonna — you know, you're not going to get any better, you just — it just results in dependency on the medication.

Clarissa's criticism of mainstream science was fundamentally compatible with Steven's, even as it was concerned less with theory and more with medicine. In dealing with the matter-spirit strain, Clarissa simultaneously identified herself as part of the countercultural spiritual movement that sees these two domains as symbolically unified.

Science and Spirituality as Synonymous

Other remarks made throughout interviews indicated an effort to discuss science and spirituality interchangeably. In these remarks, the interviewee did not so much argue why science and spirituality should be viewed non-dualistically, but simply took for granted that they were unified or synonymous. For example, Alex related the following:

I could talk about the different symbolisms that I've studied and I appreciate. Spirals are one of them. They're really powerful, and they're in everything, pretty much. They're part of your DNA, and they're part of your hair, but they're also like they're a symbol of the labyrinth, like which is like a spiritual journey . . . I mean there's different patterns, you know. You can look at the fluid, the discharge women are having when they're ovulating under a microscope, and it looks like a fern. You know, or you can — spirals, you know, they're — they occur in about everything, and um, so those are just some of the patterns. They are just really obvious if like once you're open to them. You see them everywhere, like the pattern of a spider web, or the ways trees grow and the way like rivers run look the same. I mean rivers from midway, I mean things like that. It just goes deeper and deeper and into so many different levels. And I think it's just really — it's really an intense thing, and some people can experience it. I think that's what people who are, you know, have been enlightened, have reached nirvana, I think that's what they can feel.

A measure of scientific terminology and jargon was utilized as symbolic capital to promote Alex's claim. She deftly moved from talk of "DNA" to talk of "nirvana" to resolve any strain there might be between science and spirituality. Alex asserted herself as an alternative spiritualist striving to be "open" to the interconnections she described.

Mary Lou was asked what she meant by the terms "matter" and "spirit":

Matter and spirit. Like I say, becoming discernible at the point that I think I'm doing the best work, with the, uh, uh, spirit — I guess they have to be looked at together because that's the way you framed the question. Also, that's how I look at it. They're, uh, I mean there's a hard science to matter. It's called chemistry — biochemistry. People, I — you know, like so I apply all that stuff to matter, okay? When you say, "What is matter?" Atoms, you — scientific terms. Okay, so what is matter when it's viewed in a holistic way, in this altered state that I have, you know, developed in the spirit that I feel — uh, um, it — it's such a — a comfortable leap from knowing this is a human being made of this chemistry, this is matter, I can see it, I can feel it, I've known about it, and this is individual, you know. Okay, at the same time, I know this individual has a spirit, so the spirit's what I'm going to effect, so the spirit is, um, maybe the magic behind all the balance behind the nature of the systems of the balance in that human being. And, uh, so, uh, when that, uh — when those systems are sorta out — out of balance, uh, it's a different sensation. The currents do a different kind of thing. Uh, uh, they move. The spirit — the spirit is a sense of, uh, physicality and spirituality all at one time.

Mary Lou utilized scientific references to promote her countercultural spiritual viewpoint that spirit and matter fundamentally were unified. Once again, terminologies were implemented as symbolic capital to promote alternative spirituality as viable, and to identify herself as part of this movement in her approach to science and spirituality.

Talking "Scientifically"

In addition to efforts to resolve the strain between science and spirituality per se, other comments indicated that the speaker was implementing specific strategies of scientific discourse to promote his or her countercultural spiritual beliefs and experiences. In these remarks, spiritual pursuits were viewed as "scientific" for the symbolic capital used to explain or frame them. There were three general types of these remarks: efforts to "scientifically" categorize spiritual information; anecdotes involving a kind of skeptical search for empirical "proof" of one's beliefs; and "scientific"-like analogies[3].

Classificatory

Scientific information frequently is organized into parsimonious categories (Harr 1986; Holton 1993; Gieryn 1995). Efforts to engage in "scientific" categorization appeared in nineteen interviews.

Jack was asked to describe his spiritual activities:

Mainly meditation, and, uh, uh, I — I believe in the Kundalini. I don't know if you know what that is: the energy centers in man. You know, I — I do what's called chakra cleansing every week, you know. It's pretty scientific, you know, you, uh, just meditate every day, clean your chakras every week. It's kind of like an inner bath.

When asked to explain what he meant when stating that this practice was "scientific," he replied:

It's scientific because each chakra is an energy center in man and — and you can associate several symptoms or sicknesses of man with each chakra, and you can cure physical symptoms with the cleansing of these chakras. So it does have a scientific background.

Jack alleged that his spiritual pursuits have a scientific background for the ways in which symptoms, energy centers or places on the body (i.e., "chakras") and spiritual practice can be categorically addressed. He promoted his alternative spiritual agenda by so doing, utilizing symbolic capital to address the strain between science and spirituality.

There were elements of the classificatory even in more general comments. Arthur was asked to explain what he meant by the word, "powerful":

A criteria, for me, of something being "powerful" is that it can shift me away from a normal state of consciousness easily, okay? You, uh — to feel power in something is to pick up something and be totally focused on it. Um, to — yeah, to allow and — and — be able to shift into a — another state of awareness, in part because of it, okay? Uh, a lot of things can do that, not just magical things, but magicians tend to surround themselves with objects that will evoke power to them. Uh, evoke a sense of focus. And what you do with it depends on who you are and what you're interested in. Um, you can reserve that power for yourself. You can reserve that power to be able to maintain a focus at times when you otherwise would not be focused. Um, you can use that sense of power to, um, overcome resistance of other people to ideas that you have, okay? Um, there are lots of different things you can do with it.

The word "science" is not used, but Arthur nonetheless suggested there were discreet — perhaps even objective — categories or classifications that could be made in terms of the issue at hand: who could utilize what form of power in what circumstance. This type of symbolic capital identified Arthur as a countercultural spiritualist, and advanced his agenda accordingly. A "scientific-like" strategy was employed to suggest an affinity between spirituality and empirical ways of knowing.

Seeking "Proof"

Other comments made by interviewees indicated efforts to seek empirical evidence or "proof" of one's spiritual beliefs. Using proofs is another strategy often employed by mainstream science (Gieryn 1983, 1988, 1995; Latour 1987; Hollway 1989; Bruner 1990). Such statements appeared in all twenty-two interviews.

Here is a story from Melanie:

I'd say probably about eighty percent of the time the things that you dream are trying to teach you something. Uh, it might not be a big profound lesson or something — that's probably about five percent of the time — but just little things that you need to do like daily or weekly or whatever. And the other twenty percent is, you know, weird goofy dreams and — or psychic dreams. Uh, I have a really intimate relationship with my father, he's like my best friend in the world, and he does not dream at all. When my grandfather died, I didn't even know that he was sick, and I called my dad up that night and told him about my dream. And he had never shown any belief in, you know, like dreams or anything like that and I — I — he just got — he got so quiet and my dad does not get quiet. He was really taken aback. And that happened about three years ago, and ever since then he's been like really intense, like studying Ju — Jung and dreams, and he's gone to dream workshops. And he heard from somebody, this guy out in [location], um — that he went to a workshop at that [told him that] sometimes, um, when parents don't dream, they pass on the ability to their children to dream like ten-fold, extremely vividly, and [my siblings] and myself all have incredibly vivid dreams. But I have this connection with my dad, and I'll call him up sometimes and say, you know, "Are you okay? What's goin' on? I had this dream last night, blah-blah-blah." And now he listens to me, um, and he's — it's really cool to see him grow. He's going to be [age] this year and, you know, they say you can't teach — you can't teach an old dog but it's not true at all.

Melanie's efforts to classify her dreams pointed to a form of skepticism, i.e., she was not convinced that *all* dreams were portentious. From Melanie's viewpoint, she had acquired "proof" of the validity of her experience with the otherworldly. Even her father, disinclined toward such beliefs, changed his mind. Strains between "proof" and skepticism regarding these spiritual experiences were addressed, with the spiritual perspective being favored.

Badger related a story about a spiritual commune:

People communicated with plants, and plant spirits told them actually where they wanted to be planted, and like I said, they took their own human waste and put it in the soil. It has incredible power, it — it's really scientifically proved. They were really blending the science within their religion now, and that's what I want to look at . . . You know what I mean, we need for it to really stand up. You know, I want it to be able to really stand up, and not just believe just for — just — you know, believe in something more binding. I like when there's really scientific things that come into play. And they were using a lot of seaweed, which we know is a natural source of gelidium now, which can make plants grow outrageous. You know, to twice and three times their height, and just do wild things with plants, and so the plants — but the plants told them everything to put in the garden and stuff like that. So there was like a blending, an all coming together, an energy "connecting-ness" of these energies all coming together.

Notions of talking plants were advanced simultaneously with discussions of fertilizer and scientific "proof." Once again, strains between science and spirituality were addressed in this assertion of "proof," with emphasis fundamentally on the spiritual, despite frequent references to science.

Metaphor and Analogy

Scientific explanation often utilizes metaphors or analogies to explain or simplify abstract or difficult concepts (MacCormac 1976; Burke 1989). In twenty cases, interviewees gave evidence of utilizing this strategy, once again suggesting efforts to advance alternative spirituality by drawing upon elements of scientific discourse. For example, Iris discussed what she called "greater force." I asked what she meant by this term:

Good question. Um. it's — I'll have to start by saying it's awareness. Um, at the center of every single deity there is a capital ["D"] deity. Um, I see deity as sort of like a hundred-sided dice [die]. Okay, then you've got a hundred-sided dice [die], you've got a hundred deities. But the center of gravity of that dice [die] is the absolute — is the absolute center. And you know every deity that you choose — I can't say any names — you know, every deity that you choose is yet just another facet of that central force.

A seemingly ineffable strain caused by the idea of the separateness yet interconnectedness of deities was made understandable through Iris's analogy of the die, whether or not one happens to agree with her. Her analogy suggested that Iris' spiritual worldview was cogent enough to lend itself to reducibility through metaphor. A "scientific"-like strategy was used to add credibility to her countercultural spiritual understanding of deities.

Eli explained his belief that all people are spiritually interconnected through the following metaphorical declaration:

We're all — it's not linear, you know. We're not on track where I'm here and you're here, so I'm behind you. It's like we're dots on a balloon. You inflate the balloon, the dots are moving. Each of them in a different direction. So nobody's ahead of anybody else, we're just in different places . . . Put pepper in a bowl of water. Put a piece of dish washing soap on your finger. Watch the pepper, and you'll see what I'm talking about — that tension film. That's what we're all riding on.

Complex ideas were made more comprehensible through illustration–the nature of which somewhat invokes memories of the primary school science classroom. Scientific jargon was implemented (e.g., "tension surface") to elaborate on this spiritual interconnectedness that suggested flight away from dualistic strains between matter and spirit.

Technology as Positive

All of the interviewees expressed approbation for technology. One might have predicted that alternative spiritualists would oppose technology for its being a by-product of mainstream science, but such was not the case. However, it was a guarded endorsement: technology was positive when utilized within an overriding spiritual framework.

Maria was asked to respond to the word "technology":

Technology? You know, a few years ago I would have been like, "Satan!" But now I'm just like, "Okay, fine, technology." But, um, you know, technology — it's got to be responsible. . . . [It's] getting a bad rap because it keeps falling under corporations. Technology can be me having a mystical insight that makes me invent something, you know, that's healing.

Maria conceptually subsumed technology into spirituality to such an extent that "me having a mystical insight" was technology. Criticizing mainstream corporations, she furthermore alleged that the "responsible" manner in which technology would properly be carried out involved some form of spiritual "healing." Maria's preferences as a countercultural spiritualist were made apparent in addressing the strain between technology and spirituality

Jerry spoke similarly when asked the same question:

I would like to see technology integrated more with magic, and vice versa. For a long time, I thought technology was a really horrible thing, 'cause all I was seeing was all the destruction that it caused. But lately I've realized all the really wonderful things it can do, too. So if magic and technology are integrated, then I think we'll really have something.

Jerry claimed that "magic" and technology fundamentally were compatible, thereby reconciling any strain between the two domains. In doing so, he asserted a clear preference for spirituality over pure technology. He viewed technology as having been a destructive force, and saw magic as a means to make technology a positive force instead.

CONCLUSION

Alternative spiritualists characteristically view mainstream social institutions (including mainline religions) as promoting allegedly false dualisms between matter and spirit. They see mainstream science as particularly full of such alleged dualisms. Countercultural spiritualists believe that matter and spirit ultimately are unified, and so attempt to advance a discourse that utilizes elements of science. There is a paramount sense that alternative spirituality can successfully unite science and spirituality in a way that mainline religions or mainstream science cannot. These interviewees uphold the idea that the alleged false dualism between matter and spirit is a major concern for countercultural spiritualists. Comments regarding this strain were heard frequently in interviews, and were often talked about similarly across interviewees (as per Table 3.1). This would suggest that talk about science and spirituality is another form of symbolic capital utilized by alternative spiritualists to promote alternative spirituality as an informal social movement.

Table 3.1: Frequencies of Science/Spirituality Comments in Interviews

Frequencies of Science/Spirituality Comments in Interviews	N=22	Percent of Sample
Mainstream Society as Dualistic	22	100
Mainline Religions as Dualistic	21	91
Science as Story	22	100
(Science in opening remarks)	12	55
"Correcting" Science	22	100
Science and Spirituality as Synonymous	22	100
Classificatory	19	86
Seeking "Proof"	22	100

Frequencies of Science/ Spirituality Comments in Interviews	N=22	Percent of Sample
Metaphor and Analogy	20	91
Technology as Positive	22	100

NOTES

1. Some mainline churches might disagree that they have embraced secular dualistic tendencies, noting that that which is considered the proper domain of religion often overlaps with secular social issues that are difficult to divorce from science — e.g., environmentalism, reproductive rights, and so on (Bellah 1976; Wuthnow 1985; Roof 1985; Beckford 1989; Carter 1993). Donahue (1993) found that while members of both liberal and conservative mainline Protestant denominations did not endorse such New Age beliefs as astrology or reincarnation, relatively high numbers of respondents agreed with other articulations of New Age ideology concerning self-growth or environmentalism.

2. Anthony possibly did not address mainline religions in terms of mirroring the dualisms of mainstream society. Despite the fact that he felt estranged from Catholicism for its views on his mother's divorce, he spoke highly of mainline religions when asked for his opinion of them — even though he had just finished being critical of mainstream society for its dualistic limitations.

3. These various strategies are not unknown to mainline religions, suggesting that perhaps there indeed are common overlaps between scientific and religious knowledge claims. However, alternative spiritualists are interested in utilizing aspects of science more than aspects of mainline religions (Campbell and McIver 1987), and the comments quoted herein reflect this preference.

4

Other Dualisms: Earth/Sky, Goddess/God, Dark/Light

Besides the strain between science and spirituality, alternative spiritualists frequently discuss the alleged dualistic tendencies of mainstream society along several major dimensions. As with other types of ideological declarations, this both addresses and attempts to resolve the symbolic strain at hand, while promoting countercultural spirituality as a social movement through symbolic capital. Hence, it is alleged that through alternative spirituality one can come to understand that earth is as sacred as the "sky-like" heavens, that the female image of the divine (the Goddess) is equally sacred to that of the male God, and that images or forces associated with darkness are not evil but spiritually equal to those associated with light. In sum, it is asserted that countercultural spiritualists do not make the dualistic errors that other people often do, whereby one is able to acquire an holistic approach to spirituality.[1]

EARTH AS SPIRITUAL

Alternative spiritualists state that problems of the earthly realm are incorrectly not treated holistically — as involving spirit as well as matter. Drawing upon contemporary environmentalist rhetoric as well as older spiritual traditions that honored the earth as sacred (including Native American traditions), activities involving the earth and protection of the earth have been conceptualized as spiritual (Bellah 1976; Wuthnow 1976; Stone 1978; Adler 1986; Starhawk 1989; Bednarowski 1991; Allen 1992; McGaa 1992).

For example, in a recent issue of *Shaman's Drum: A Journal of Experiential Shamanism,* there were articles about transpersonal powers and spirit guides, but also ones dealing with legislation banning the slaughter of the Alaskan wolf and protection of natural areas that developers wish to exploit. In a featured interview with a Western Shoshone Elder, Corbin Harney, issues such as pollution and the political movement to ban nuclear testing from Western Shoshone lands are discussed. At the same time, Harney asserted that "everything has spirit" (White 1995:32) and that "Water likes to talk to us" (White 1995:33). Thus, a mystical spirituality was offered alongside straightforward environmentalist information.

At spiritual festivals and fairs, alongside information tables regarding one's past lives or astrological chart there were environmentally related petitions, and workshops in organic gardening, solar energy, wind power and how to design ecologically friendly houses. Group rituals were enacted to remind the participants of the sacredness of the earth. At an instructional lecture on Wiccan beliefs, someone asked how the novice might start studying witchcraft. The speaker replied that the best way was to start growing plants. He stated that even just growing a geranium on a windowsill would familiarize a person with the earth's cycles of growth. Putting fingers in the soil would enable a person to begin to feel connected to spiritual powers.

Highly compatible sentiments apparently had been internalized by my interviewees. Even had I formally hypothesized that environmentalism would be a topic mentioned, I could not have predicted the extent to which it was featured in the interviews when individuals were simply asked to discuss their spirituality. Every person I interviewed made continual references to regarding the earth as sacred and/or the need for more environmental consciousness.

Environmentalist Self Story

In eighteen out of twenty-two cases, environmental concerns were a major theme that permeated the entire interview. For example, Badger had been practicing yoga for ten years. I might have anticipated that he would emphasize this practice in his self story, perhaps beginning by sharing how he met his first yoga teacher. Instead, he began as follows:

Our surroundings tell a lot about us, our appearance[s] tell about our spirituality and how everything is connected in. You know, the diet, belief system — uh, you know, everything pretty much. The way you work, and the — every step you take being that important as a spiritual path. And, uh, too many people, I think, separate their normal life and don't think about what their job means every day [and] how much it really means, where we're at right now. And, uh, uh, I — I, um, thought a lot about what's real. When I'd look around me in the city and just see everything man-made, synthetic, and then think about what's real when I'm in the woods is just different plants, the ground. As I later learned, [where I live now], where I knew water is clean, the air is clean, it really feels right, the land is really abounding with life, which, when you can go up to a creek and see things that are living in it, you know the water is fairly clean. And where I came from in [state], it stinks like a sewer and there's — everything's dead in there and stuff. Uh, you know — you know — you know it's real when you taste your water and it tastes right, and the air: you can really feel it when it rains — you know, the smell when it rains, and — and, uh, the bio-energy from the trees.

Badger's discourse never strayed far from issues such as pollution and how to take better care of the earth. That these topics were central to spirituality would appear to have been deeply ingrained within him; he never explained why clean drinking water or the "bio-energy" of the trees were spiritual, but assumed the connection to be self-evident. He continually attempted to resolve the symbolic strain between matter (i.e., earth) and spirit, and the alleged false dualism thereof. Simultaneously, he was outspoken in advancing his counter-cultural spiritual agenda — a pollution-free environment that would be obtained through spiritual awareness.

Clarissa began her story like this:

I was brought up Episcopalian, and that really turned me off to religion in a big way. Um, the church that I went to was like really hypocritical. The things I remember that were good were like this, um, [religious] camp that we went to and it was out in nature, called [name], which actually is about [number of] miles from here. And there was like an outside church with an altar and benches and, um, that was like one of my favorite memories. I loved it. I thought like that was the best way to worship, 'cause that was church to me. Even when I was a kid, I thought like church should be outside because you're worshipping nature, and that's what God is supposed to be . . . Just the whole idea of like the cycle of life and worshipping nature and honoring those things that you eat, whether it be like lettuce or buffalo, and — and realizing that you should, uh, respect every aspect of your life, every piece of land that you rest your food on is sacred, because that helps you to live, and you have that to live. And I see such disrespect in organized religions.

In stating her belief that worship of God should rightfully focus upon nature and the earth, Clarissa also advanced her view of organized religion, which she felt to be "hypocritical" for its lack of understanding. Her alternative spiritual viewpoint regarding the sacredness of the earth was the standard by which other religious pursuits were judged.

Earth and Spirituality Synonymous

Another manner of speaking in interviews was to deftly switch from discussing spirituality to discussing environmentalism — and then back again. This type of discursive move occurred in twenty of the interviews.

Clarissa was explaining that she believed that forests are "spiritual" places when she launched into the following:

Rainforests are just being cut down, and like the size of — every — every second like the size of a football field is cut down in the rain forest, and I mean it's just like we're killing the earth, kind of. You know, and people don't realize what they're doing. Like all the — there's so many medicinal parts, so many — I mean, so many species of plants are eliminated, they go extinct every day, and they don't even know what they're killing off. You know, there could be a cure for AIDS, you know, that — that just went extinct today, or something, you know. It's just crazy. And the — the species of animals. I believe that everything has a spirit: trees, animals, you know, and I just have a lot of respect for the earth, and I try to honor that and take care of it. And I kind of view her as my mother, you know, the source of all life.

After discussing a possible loss of a cure for AIDS, Clarissa asserted that "everything has a spirit — trees, animals," whereby the earth itself takes on a spiritual dimension, personified as "my mother" and the "source of all life."[2] Her environmentalist stance was referred to interchangeably with her spiritual beliefs. In this way, she strove to resolve the strain between the two domains while advocating saving the rain forests.

The following assertion came from Mary Lou:

Real power is when you have that sense of matter and spirit, such as being in nature, when you — you're able to be in the moment, and at the same time, use that energy, that power. You can take just a single blade of grass, or be with the animals — the forces. Which is why it's — it's not really science when people destroy things, destroy the earth, because science is — should be about respecting life. That's real logic. Matter and spirit. The awareness of the physical that spiritually heals. It's matter, but it's beyond matter. Being in nature and — and being in the spirit.

Much of Mary Lou's spiritual quest has been to reckon between the alleged dualism of matter and spirit, as evidenced by this passage. The symbolic strain between the two domains was dealt with in such a way as to refer to matter and spirit synonymously. Mary Lou promoted her countercultural spiritual agenda and criticized elements of mainstream society.

Environmental Knowledge as Spiritual Knowledge

Acquiring knowledge of the earth was depicted as having been important insofar as advancing one's overriding spiritual understanding. Environmental knowledge was depicted as spiritual knowledge in nineteen of the interviews.

Flora talked about how participation at a spiritual festival was instrumental in her making a commitment to spiritual pursuits. After discussing meaningful encounters with certain individuals and participation in rituals, she went on to convey the following:

The other thing at that earth mysteries gathering that had happened was the promotional material for [it] that talked about the earth, talked about how we were raping the earth, and covering her in pavement. And I made a really deep connection with the earth, or with Gaia, or whatever you want to call the consciousness that is this planet that we live on.

A key factor in this festival's importance to Flora was the "promotional material that talked about the earth," which was being "raped" by humankind. This led her to make "a really deep connection with the earth," which would seem to be vital in the overall framework of her spirituality. She framed environmentalist discourse within a spiritual context. Once again, a strain between earth and the sacred was addressed and potentially resolved, and an environmentalist agenda within a spiritual framework was promoted at the same time.

Anthony identified the following anecdote as being significant in his spiritual development:

A [Native American] shaman came down — a, um, sort of a crazy wisdom shaman came down from [place], and I was in a sweat lodge with him, and uh, it was just — it was the hottest sweat lodge I'd ever done. He put in maybe thirteen stones at one point. . . . Just that commitment to spirit, and that through — he was talking about suffering, that we're going to suffer, and now we're in for it, and it was so hot in there that you literally couldn't breathe and you couldn't see and your skin was burning, and that that is part of his tradition that if you go though that experience, that it is e benefit to those outside. And his wisdom — it was like talking about nature, talking about the cycles of the earth, and about suffering, and how the earth renews itself when — it's — because the change of seasons involves suffering. Just that balance of suffering and celebration that it is nature and the world and life, and how to save the earth, things we need to know every day in our lives to save the earth. It's extra work, its suffering to — to take steps to preserve the world we live in. But it's a — it's a — also a celebration.

Besides appreciating the intense experience of the sweat lodge itself,[3] Anthony also felt he gained information about the earth that was spiritual information. In addressing the strain between earth and spirit, he advanced the cause of environmentalism, and exemplified how alternative spiritualists address it.

Alternative Spiritual Community and Environmentalism

In sixteen instances, interviewees spoke of the countercultural spiritual community at large as an arena that emphasizes environmental concerns, and this in and of itself figured into its appeal for the speaker at hand. Here is how Ralph described the alternative spiritual movement:

It's like coming back to the earth, coming back to what Native Americans were all about — you know, living in oneness and harmony with the universe, not in disconnection with it, and it's like, uh, it's — it's a celebration of just, you know, for the earth, to give the earth thanks for all the things it gives us, you know, that we don't really even think about. You know, lots of people don't think about where lots of things came from, like steel in the cars, rubber, you know — if it wasn't for the earth, you know, we wouldn't have any of these things, and it's pretty much just getting back to the earth. To give back and give thanks to the earth, and be more of that one community, for that one, you know that oneness. That community that people are looking for.

Countercultural spirituality can be seen as "coming back to the earth." Ralph did not say, for example, that spirituality is for "going to heaven." Such a viewpoint would not be reflective of "harmony" and "oneness," a sacred sense of non-dualistic interconnectedness. References to steel and rubber for cars are located within a spiritual context, i.e., things of the earth being offered "celebration" and "thanks." Ultimately, such things are part of a larger, highly desired spiritual community. Ralph attempted to reckon with a strain between matters of the earth and matters of the sacred, and to assert the values of alternative spirituality simultaneously.

Jesse had an elaborate belief system regarding his being one of many entities brought to earth for specific reasons. Part of the story he told went as follows:

My purpose in being alive on the earth is to re-green the planet. To re-green and contribute to the genetic diversity. [My people] want to bring the forest back to life, to plant trees and grow food and learn the magic of the seasons and the cycles. Use wizardry to harness the elements for energy. Wind power. Solar power. To re-green and terra-form the world. To get away from the people who want to stop the knowledge or hide it for themselves.

Jesse discussed his identity as a countercultural spiritualist as emphasizing environmentalism, criticizing mainstream society in the process.

Environmental Action as Spiritual Action

Sixteen interviewees listed some form of specific environmental action as being an explicitly spiritual activity. To cite an example: Jerry lived in an environmentally-sensitive, alternative setting that advocated education regarding safe countercultural forms of energy. He helped organize workshops and distributed literature on these issues. While Jerry frequently participates in spiritual rituals, he did not do so on any regular basis:

I don't do very much actual ceremony unless it's with a group of friends where we want to get together and, say, like tomorrow [sic] for the summer solstice. I'll get together with some people around a bonfire and we'll be thinking about the sun and just celebrating the coming of summer and all that. But it's — I don't think I do anything necessarily special that's spiritual because as much as I can I try to make everything I do part of my spirituality. [I probe as to how he does this.] I have it very easy living at [residence], because the idea of [this place] is pretty much what I've always wanted to do. So it's made it real easy for me to sort of — I live there and work for the community, and my aim is to make [this place], um, completely self-sufficient, and just live completely by the natural cycle, not by any outside influence.

I asked Jerry if he could illustrate this more specifically, for example, how would going to the post office for stamps be a spiritual activity for him? He laughed, as if I could not have picked a better example, and said:

Well, when I do that, I can just — because one of my jobs with [place of residence] is taking care of the mail, answering the requests for information and stuff, so that makes it easy.

Jerry demonstrated how even a seemingly mundane action like going to the post office for stamps takes on spiritual significance for him. But this spiritual significance stemmed from the fact that he was conveying not just spiritual information to others by going to the post office, but information related to his environmental activist stance. He attempted to resolve the strain between the sacred and the mundane, as well as to advance his personal agenda in this regard.

Alex conveyed the following:

Uh, I guess it's [spirituality] not something that I really go to church for. It's not like — I don't go somewhere, and it's not like that is the time I set aside to be spiritual. It's nothing like that. It's more like in every — I think about it constantly, you know, and it — it's something I try to — it's not — I try to keep it as un — as undogmatic as possible, like no — no weird like — like if I do this, this is gonna happen, and oh, I haveta keep doing this, you know, and — or anything like that. It's more of just what I feel — what feels good and right. Like I don't feel comfortable throwing trash, you know, out in the forest, 'cause I think that's really disrespectful to the things around me.

Not unlike Jerry, Alex sees spirituality in terms of ongoing actions more than finite rituals. And again like Jerry, she picked an environmentalist action as being representative of her ongoing quest for spirituality — in her case, to be careful not to litter in the forest.

Earth-Based Experience as Spiritual

Additionally, for all the interest in pursuits such as reincarnation or the Tarot, often interviewees spoke of simple experiences in nature as being among their most profound — perhaps the most profound — moments in their spiritual journeys. In this way, interviewees further asserted that the spiritual realm does not exist apart from the earth (as some might dualistically believe). And since the earth is spiritual, it is something to be honored and respected. In fact, this type of remark showed up in eighteen out of twenty-two interviews.

Salient instances of these statements often occurred towards the end of the interview process, when I asked each interviewee to give an example of an especially important spiritual experience he/she had had. Eli had acquired many years of experience with Wiccan rituals (and was something of a "walking ency-clopedia" of information in this regard). Yet he surprisingly answered this question as follows:

I was sitting on a hilltop several years ago. It was about 12 years ago, and I was watching a moonrise, and at the same time I was watching the moonrise, I was listening to a deer in an oak thicket behind and to the right of me. And that moment became so powerful that I felt fixed. I had another moment like that with a bird, and once when I heard wolves it occurred to me that I had a voice, and I felt very aware of the God energy — the Goddess energy — at once, and aware of how inextricably they were in me. And at those moments, I just felt fixed in the universe, and who I [really] am.

To Eli, seemingly simple moments in nature portended "powerful" energy indicative of "God" or "Goddess" energy that made him feel "fixed in the uni-verse" and in touch with his true self. For all of his knowledge of intricate spiri-tual rituals, it was these simple, earth-based experiences that stirred him the most profoundly. For the earth itself would seem to be highly spiritual; human-made rituals presumably would be less compelling. Thus, Eli addressed a strain between earth and spirit, and also promoted his alternative spiritual agenda that emphasized the sacredness of the earth.

Discussion of nature as integral to one's spiritual worldview occurred else-where in the interviews. Laurel discussed early intimations of spirituality in her childhood. These experiences included early "psychic responses" that her par-ents later shared with her, such as her seeming ability to sense when the phone would ring when she was a baby. But these experiences also included the fol-lowing with her mother:

She spent a lot of time out in the woods, and on nature studies. She's very intelligent, she's like a self-taught naturalist. And I remember she used to take me out like in this pine forest just north of where we lived, and she'd say, "This is God's cathedral. This is where you can connect with spirit the most." And, uh, so we would spend hours on like rock piles down by the river, just going through all the textures and colors. And, um, she also believed in — in UFOs very much, and, uh, [location] is a good place to see interesting things in the sky at night, and, uh, you know it — we'd watch that occasionally.

For Laurel and her mother, it was in nature that one can "connect with God the most," not in a literal "cathedral." Once one made this connection to the earth, interconnecting with the cosmos of the sky — here expressed as "UFOs" — was the next logical step. Laurel made an effort to resolve a certain strain between earth and spirit, as well as to advocate her personal agenda, which simultaneously concerned the validity of her spiritual experiences and the fundamental sacredness of the earth.

THE GODDESS MOVEMENT

Another important ideological strain that was addressed in interviews posited the alleged existence of the female Goddess alongside the male God. The Goddess movement is claimed to offer self-empowerment through an articulation of the female experience as divine, and to protest what are perceived to be patriarchal values that promote gender inequalities. This ideology is enacted ritualistically, yet also involves feminist ideology that can be applied beyond the ritual setting (Adler 1986; Christ 1987; Englesman 1987; Starhawk 1989; Allen 1992; Neitz 1994; Griffin 1995). The persons I interviewed were not exclusively aligned with the Goddess movement, but all had been exposed to it. As with their approach to other forms of religion or spirituality, interviewees felt free to incorporate elements of Goddess worship into their overriding spiritual worldview.

The Goddess and Women: Seeking Equality

Each of the eleven of the women I interviewed made positive reference to the Goddess as empowering the self as a woman, and fighting sexism in society at large. For example, consider remarks made by Gypsy, who began her story by telling me her mother's advice when, as a child, she first announced she wanted to explore different religions:

The one recommendation my mother had put on all this was that, um, to find out how they feel — felt about women with their religions, and so I said, "Oh well, that's fair enough, I'm a woman, you know." And so, whenever you go to a church the priest or something always wants to welcome you like, "Oh, come on in, please come back, da-da-da-da-da." So I'd always ask him. He'd be like, "Do you have any questions?" and I'd — I'd go, "What role do women have?" And every time it seemed like they were stumbling over their words and they didn't really know how to tell this ten-year-old girl that in most of those religions, they [women] were a lesser vessel, and they weren't quite as important as men, and, um, I never felt like I got a comfortable answer from any of them, or that they had any belief in what they were saying about women.

A sociopolitical concern for gender equality was linked to Gypsy's individual pursuit of a spirituality. She made this connection by promoting counter-cultural spirituality through criticism of mainline religions. However, none of the women I interviewed considered themselves to be feminist separatists, or exclusive Goddess worshippers; they also sought to honor and pursue non-Goddess forms of spirituality. Thus, while she found mainline religions patriarchal, Gypsy also stated:

It wasn't that I thought that women were better, but I thought that the female aspect needs to be worked on more now, because of how much the masculine influence has had that we need a push towards the female. Not that they're more important once again, but to balance out the last 2,000 years [laughter].

Ultimately, Gypsy sought "balance" by emphasizing male and female conceptualizations of the divine, as opposed to labeling the divine as genderless. She promotes her agenda in this regard while addressing the strain per se. (Later, when asked to comment on the word "God," she replied, "Part of the whole." When asked to comment on the word "Goddess," she replied, "Part of the whole."[4])

Alex expressed a similar viewpoint:

After awhile, I had a friend who got me interested in the Goddess religions and earth mother religions, sort of a female-like power. The earth energy that is everywhere and everything, and, um, so I started — I don't know — I started reading more about that, and it just — it really interested me in a way as being a woman, and the fact that there have been like paintings in caves, like statues and a lot of artifacts have been found life from twenty-five or thirty thousand years ago like that give people good reason to believe in Goddess religion with ancient humans, you know, much more than Christianity. So I thought that was pretty cool.

Alex was intrigued by the notion of a "female-like power." But she also stated:

For me, I guess, when I say "the Goddess," I mean like it's not really a deity I speak of, or some like woman, you know, in the sky, or something. It's more like — it's more like an energy, and it encompasses, you know, not just female energy, but male energy and it — and it's a nice balance. And it encompasses different aspects of people.

Alex did not view the Goddess as exclusively feminine as it also encompassed "male energy," making for "a nice balance" that one could achieve as an alternative spiritualist. Once again, gender strains were not eliminated so much as addressed symbolically to create a cohesive whole.

In sum, the women I interviewed spoke of Goddess spirituality as a means of obtaining gender equality and self-validation by having a female image of the divine with which to identify. But they did not exclude the possibility of the male image as divine. The alleged dualism between male and female was acknowledged, and balance was sought by honoring both — rather than advocating androgyny per se.[5]

The Goddess and Men: Seeking Nurturance

The eleven men I interviewed similarly saw "Goddess" within a larger framework of "balance." Certain attributes were conceptualized as male or female, but both categories were deemed necessary for holistic spirituality.[6]

However, comments made by men about the Goddess also differed from those made by women. Only five of the eleven men mentioned the Goddess without first being prompted to do so. While the women interviewees spoke of the Goddess in terms of larger gender inequalities, the men I interviewed spoke of the Goddess more as an expressive or nurturing force that aided one's immediate self.

More than any of the men I interviewed, Jack discussed a deep personal connection with the Goddess. He was also the only man who talked about the Goddess in terms of large-scale gender inequalities. Feeling isolated from his peers at a crucial phase in his life, he found it difficult to accept the male God of his Catholic upbringing. For when he could not "love" the people who were being cruel to him, he felt that this male God would want to "punish" him. When asked why he felt more comfortable with the "Goddess" than with "God," Jack replied as follows:

See, that's the problem I have with a male kind of God, because, um, for centuries, men have been dominant and women have been, um, subversive in society. And I really don't think that God is a male or a female, but I like more the idea of a God who is nurturing than a God who is avenging, and I like more the idea of a God who is protective and who has female qualities than of a God who is male and has, uh, uh, attacking qualities, and, uh, you know, war qualities.

Although he stated that ultimately God did not have a gender, Jack associated male concepts of deity with dominance of men over women, as well as with "war qualities." But he associated the Goddess with the more "nurturing" and "protective qualities." While women said they appreciated the Goddess because it enabled them to feel not excluded from the divine, Jack utilized the Goddess more for healing and nurturing.

This concept of the Goddess as being nurturing sometimes was expressed as a more explicit form of assistance. Arthur described a spiritual exercise in which the following occurred:

I evoked a, uh — an energy that I later identified as the Goddess of Ishtar. Uh, the Sumerian Babylonian Goddess of Ishtar. At least that was how I identified it. I told you, I don't know if it's the same one, 'cause it's speaking English to me. And I started talking to her in terms of a priestess. Uh, she said she wanted me to have a child, and I said, "Well, in order for me to have a child, I have to have a priestess, I have to have somebody to actually do the workings with. And — but I said, "I'm willing to make this deal. I'm willing to offer you the child if you will offer me a priestess."

In conveying this information, Arthur did not pause to explain to the listener that a deity can be female; it was simply a given. He did not feel awkward, as a male, in dealing with a female spiritual presence. In fact, Arthur began the story of meeting the woman who was to become his wife and the mother of their child (i.e., his "priestess") by framing this major life event around a female, not a male, deity. Yet, he regarded this deity as an equal with whom he could negotiate a "bargain." The Goddess did not provide spiritual identification or gender empowerment (as with the women), but assisted Arthur in achieving his goal.

In sum, the men (like the women) spoke of certain qualities as being male or female, and of seeking a balance between the two. But they spoke of the Goddess less in terms of patriarchal biases or self-empowerment, and more in terms of how the Goddess served some sort of expressive or nurturing function in their lives.

DARKNESS AS POSITIVE

Besides frequently being considered synonymous the earth or Mother Earth, the Goddess sometimes overlaps with — or is viewed as compatible with — conceptualizations of darkness versus light. Older religions frequently took for granted such things as moon cycles being connected to the different aspects of the Goddess. Such associations signified different aspects of the life experience, with the darker ones symbolic of fears or mysteries of the unknown (Adler 1986; Starhawk 1989; Griffin 1995). In this context, it is not difficult to see why those who practice magic can feel an affinity with the Goddess — or why mainstream conceptualizations of light versus dark are viewed as unduly limiting in comparison.

But whether directly spoken of in terms of the Goddess or not, there is a generalized ideology among many countercultural spiritualists concerning the limited, bifurcated conception of "darkness" as seen in Western, mainline tradition. According to this emerging line of thought (which is, once again, a synthesis of old and new ideas), that which is "dark" is not "evil," and to associate darkness with evil is racist. Instead, it is noted that that which is dark brings its own necessary life forces. For example, soil makes it possible for plants to grow, and the nightfall brings an opportunity for replenishing rest (Baltazar 1973). What is required, according to this conceptualization, is a *balance* between the dark and the light, as often typified by Native American traditions (Gill 1987; Hultkrantz 1987).

In practical terms, "darkness" and "light" become metaphors for aspects of self-exploration. As Joy (1993:22) stated, the "darker aspects" include "not only those things that, from conventional moral perspectives, are regarded as 'evil' or 'wrong.' They also include any aspect of our natural being that is not acceptable to our conscious sense of self." Thus, in the broadest sense, explorations into unresolved past conflicts, or the more disturbing emotions such as fear and anger, or guilt-free sexual expression, might all be considered metaphorical "journeys into the dark side."

In popular magazines, it is not uncommon to find references to this dualism. In the Summer 1995 issue of *Gnosis: A Journal of the Western Inner Traditions*, one reads of "chaos magic," the practitioners of which were described as follows:

Along with a general acceptance of deconstructionism, they seem to be fascinated with the shadow self, the dark spheres of reality, the phatasmagoric, macabre imagery. Not coincidentally, many Chaos magicians cut their teeth on fantasy games like Dungeons and Dragons, and many are also devotees of H. P. Lovecraft and other writers of the horror and fantasy genres. . . . This enchantment with the dark side of existence is explained by author Mishlen Linden, who observes that Western occultism has emphasized the "Gods of light," and in the process has repressed the shadow forces of the psyche. Linden declares that a balance of both light and dark images are necessary, and notes that "when both light and dark . . . have been integrated, then may we all be truly free." (Houston 1995:57)

Thus, images of the dark were linked to elements of the self as well as of the spirit, and were viewed not as evil but as that which the Western tradition has taught people to disavow, thereby dogmatically limiting possibility.

These sentiments were reflected in the interviews. In fact, a total of seventeen interviewees made at least one, and possibly two, kind(s) of reference to darkness as important to spiritual growth. As with other forms of dualism, it was alleged that there was a symbolic separation between light and dark, but that spiritual holism required addressing both aspects — as opposed to saying things like, "There is no light or dark, only gray."

Darkness in General Worldview

In fifteen cases, interviewees discussed a general viewpoint that one had to spiritually embrace both darkness and light. For example, Ralph conveyed the following:

Whenever there's light, you know, whenever there's something good there's gonna be something bad, so [you] can realize there's something good. And, uh, you know, there's — I didn't always accept that because I'd go to a festival — you know, say a mind, body and spirit festival, and there'd be a guy outside with this sign saying, "Hellfire, you're all gonna burn in hell," you know, and I didn't understand that for a long time. And then I figured that there has to be a duality in everything, you know. There has to be a dark so you can see the light — to realize that there is a light.

In articulating his ideological stance on the issue of darkness and light, Ralph also promoted alternative spirituality as having a more sophisticated grasp of these concepts than the more "Hellfire" type of individual. (Indeed, one might note that Ralph was attending a "mind, body and spirit" festival when coming to these realizations, once again ideologically suggesting resolution of symbolic strain.)

The following reflection from Laurel was similar:

I don't believe in avoiding, um, the negative, or the dark. I believe in walking into it and knowing it. But I think you do have to have a life line, and you do have to have inner ground. And perhaps losing all sense of inner ground is part of it, too . . . I had a book, um, by a Jungian analyst on alchemy, and there's — the phase you go through . . . where everything looks dark and stark and bleak. And then the other side — I forget what it's called — but it's, um, everything's bright and idealized. And you bring the two together, and they have all the colors and the textures. The mandella. That's what I'm shooting for [laughter].

The symbolic strain between light and dark was addressed by Laurel, who proceeded to offer her solution to the strain, which was to "bring the two together," and not impose dualistic limitations.

Darkness and Personal Experience

In fourteen different interviews, anecdotes were conveyed that made specific reference to the notion that one must address spiritual darkness for spiritual growth. Maria's story provided a good a example:

I started exploring my issues about, you know, why was I born into this family, what is the significance of all that stuff. So that dark work was real — led into um, also my healer, the healer within, and, um, [I] knew that I couldn't afford the pricey healers, the pricey workshops, the, you know, the big pricey things, like [name] school, and you know, all this other stuff. . . . So I basically decided I was going to be my own medicine woman. I was gonna — I was gonna, uh, somehow be objective enough to a actually work on healing, and bringing the healing power into my life. . . . The real peak of the dark stuff happened shortly after I moved to [name of place]. It was a — a lot more playful up to that time, because I started working with rocks and making mandellas and intuitively just exploring, um, tools that I had no idea what they meant. You know, just doing rock formations in my house and [not] even knowing that, oh, that's like an ancient practice, you know?

According to Maria, challenging or "dark" aspects of her life became a source of spiritual growth. In conveying this story, she also launched a critique against "pricey" workshops more indicative of mainstream, profit-motivated pursuits. The journey into symbolic darkness was viewed as part of a larger spiritual direction in her life, and in dealing with the strain between suffering and healing Maria also promoted herself as an autonomous self-healer nonetheless engaging in "ancient practices" known to others. In sum, the countercultural spiritual approach to spirituality was advanced.

Not only could facing one's "darkness" prove to be positive, but such an approach was familiar enough to some people not to even be perceived as stressful. Arthur stated the following as indication of this perspective:

The shadow side is often the side that people fear — uh, it can encompass really dark kinds of stuff. Uh, evil, demonic, okay? But it isn't necessarily bad. Uh, often what it is, it's dark because it's emerging, and it's dark and fearful because you don't understand it. Whew! Boy! Let me give you an example. Years ago, uh, at one of the art fairs, there was a woman who had some ceramic material there who — the material was just incredible. I walked by it, and just felt myself pulled over to it, and I spent much of the festival coming back there, looking at the stuff, you know, buying this, buying — you know, I'd go and buy something, and then I'd go away and then I'd buy something else. And I noticed that many of the other people in the Neo-Pagan community, uh, especially the more serious people, would also come back, and were doing exactly the same thing. We kept hovering about this person, and she was like bewildered. She — she — I remember her almost in tears, saying, "Do you really like this stuff?" And we said yes, and she said, "Some people say that it's evil." And — and I kind of stopped and I looked at it, and I felt the power that was in it. The images, they were very bizarre, but very suggestive of — of real deep subconscious stuff. Very powerful. And — and it struck me that this was very dark work, very shadow kind of work, but there — there was nothing evil about it at all, it was just hidden power, and people were responding to the power in it.

In conveying this anecdote, Arthur identifies himself as one who can get beyond the simplistic strain between darkness and light, and furthermore promotes the alternative spiritual community as being able to do so.

CONCLUSION

Not only do large-scale events and articles in popular literature promote a spiritual agenda regarding sky and earth, God and Goddess, and light and dark, but individuals who pursue countercultural spirituality will bring up these matters of their own volition. These statements suggest a possible major source of commonalty for these individuals, as seen in Table 4.1. These symbolic strains provide further communication resources for alternative spiritualists to challenge what they perceived to be the limitations and controls of mainstream society.

Interestingly, often people seemed to gain utility from the symbolic, dualistic strain at hand, and did not attempt to bypass it altogether. For example, interviewees did not say, "God has no gender," but rather spoke in terms of there being both God and Goddess. They did not say, "There is no light or dark," but instead utilized both concepts to offer what was perceived to be a

Table 4.1: Frequencies of Other Dualisms in Interviews

Frequencies of Other Dualisms in Interviews	N=22	Percent of Sample
EARTH/SKY	22	100
Environmentalist Self-Story	18	82
Earth and Spirituality Synonymous	20	91
Environmental Knowledge as Spiritual Knowledge	19	86
Alternative Spiritual Community and Environmentalism	16	73
Environmental Actions as Spiritual Actions	16	73
Earth-Based Experience as Spiritual	18	82
GODDESS/GOD	22	100
Women Seeking Equality	22	100
Men Seeking Nurturance	21	91
DARKNESS/LIGHT	17	77
Darkness in General Worldview	15	68
Darkness and Personal Experience	15	68

spiritual whole. The mainstream was depicted as having only half the pieces of the proverbial puzzle, but the pieces it had were seen as rightfully *part* of the puzzle. Mainstream sentiments and symbols were conceptually realigned, but not wholly discarded.

NOTES

Excerpts from this chapter appeared in a somewhat different form in *Sociology of Religion: A Quarterly Review*, Vol. 55 (No. 2) pgs 181-190 "Counterculturalists' Perceptions of the Goddess". Other excerpts from this chapter have been published in a somewhat different form in *Review of Religious Research* Vol. 40 (No. 1); pgs 55-73. "Alternative Spirituality and Environmentalism".

1. Kanagy and Nelsen (1995) found that contrary to popular assumptions, religious orientation did not significantly predict whether or not an individual supported environmental concerns, once one considered variables such as education level, or framed the argument in terms of issues such as federal spending. One can only speculate about how persons with an alternative spiritual orientation would fare using this measure.

2. Earth-based elements of alternative spirituality are frequently linked to issues concerning the spiritual "Goddess," whereby the female is spiritually empowered alongside the male. This notion bears feminist implications. Goodin (1992) notes that environmentalism, or "green politics," often provides a discursive framework for a shared political agenda that encompasses other issues, such as sexism.

3. Alternative spiritual gatherings frequently involve tribal-based traditions such as sweat lodges. Tents are erected with a pit in the center for the placing of rocks heated in a campfire. Participants huddle inside. Water is sprinkled on the rocks to create hot steam while invoking rituals or prayers.

4. Indeed, when conducting follow-up interviews, Gypsy took me to task for overemphasizing her Goddess-based roots, and underemphasizing her ultimate concern with spiritual balance between the female and the male.

5. Given that I am male, it is possible to consider that some women might have been altering their beliefs for my benefit. However, each of the women I interviewed frequently participated in spiritual activities open to both sexes that seemed to reflect the viewpoint they shared with me.

6. The one possible exception here was Steven, who said that he felt much Goddess spirituality was essentially a political agenda disguised as a spiritual one. Yet he was not troubled by the notion of there *being* Goddesses — in fact, he believed that different entities across different religious and spiritual traditions do literally exist, and are not mere manifestations of psychological states of being: "I don't ascribe to the idea of one great Goddess. I subscribe to the idea of many." He was not troubled by the notion of there being Goddesses who serve perfectly valid functions per se, merely that the way it was popularly applied did not meet his criteria for spiritual rigor.

5

Ideological Limitations

No single ideology has omnipotent explanatory power, and so our commitment to any one ideology is never absolute. Competing claims need to, and do, persist as influences in our lives. Such is the case despite the frequent tendency to articulate a given ideological claim as if it *were* omnipotent, and/or the only one that engages our interest (Simmel 1955; du Preez 1980; Cormack 1992).

Judging from comments made during interviews, it appears that alternative spiritualists are somewhat aware of the limitations of their ideological claims — despite the enthusiasm with which they advance them. Interviewees sometimes made remarks that took the form of acknowledging competing claims outright. In other instances, interviewees freely admitted that there were limitations in pursuing countercultural spirituality.

However, such acknowledgments did not appear to diminish the individual's commitment to alternative spirituality. Contradictions or discrepancies between spiritual and mainstream beliefs were often taken for granted. These contradictions were considered a workable and interesting part of the situation being explored (Proudfoot 1977, 1985). Unresolved issues might be seen as more a source of conflict or disbelief for the outside critic than the believer (McGuire 1988).

Therefore, when interviewees frequently admitted to limitations in being an alternative spiritualist, they were able to do so in ways that suggested ideological strain yet also promoted personal interests. Talk of limitations can be viewed as still another form of symbolic capital in this informal social movement.

ACCEPTANCE OF MAINSTREAM SOCIETY

Living in the Mainstream

No one I interviewed had illusions that their spirituality was powerful enough to instantly change mainstream society — or indeed, necessarily change it at all. Instead, all twenty-two people emphasized utilizing their spirituality to adapt as best they could to all that they did not like about mainstream society. In one form or another, this type of comment appeared in each of the interviews.

Iris, who had earlier remarked that it was "not an easy task" for her "to function on a material and spiritual plane at the same time," elaborated on this viewpoint when sharing her opinion of mainstream society:

You know, Carlos Castanada talks about functioning in all worlds, and, uh, there's got to be places for us in the mainstream society in one form or another. Um, that's kind of the way we've set ourselves up. You know, we can sit here and whine and moan about how unfair it is that we have to go humble ourselves before an employer and get paid to feed ourselves, to put a roof over our head, to pay rent, and [it] becomes like an endless cycle, but who set it up? We humans did, you know, and it's true all over the world, and it's more — it's becoming true even for the third world countries. That there's — that they need to do something that's valuable in the international market. I think that it is hard for spiritual people to find out what their marketable talent is. You know, what can I, as a shaman, offer [a] university? You know, not a whole lot. Nothing that they would pay me for, except maybe this information, you know, but, um, it's very hard. This is a one-time thing; it's not gonna happen very often. Um, what can I, as a practitioner of Kundalini, offer [a major] bank?

Iris did not appear to be promoting her spiritual viewpoint any less for noting this strain between mainstream everyday reality and her spiritual ideals. In fact, she suggested that it was spiritual (as per Castanada) to be "functioning in all worlds." When asked if he experienced daily life obstacles to his beliefs, Jerry answered:

I have a real big obstacle with my spiritual beliefs, and that's society. And I just have to deal with it, because I could either not be connected to it at all, but that's almost next to impossible without leaving the planet. 'Cause even if I were to just go into a national forest, that's still connected to Babylon, and it's kind of hard for me to deal with. But then again, I try to use it as best I can, and try to take advantage of its conveniences.

Jerry likened the mainstream world to "Babylon," thereby conceptualizing it within spiritual terms — symbolically subsuming it within his countercultural spiritual frame of reference. He stated he had made peace with the limitations imposed by mainstream society, and so doing apparently did not compel him to stop promoting his spiritual viewpoint as preferable when addressing the strain between the two worlds.

Mainstream and Alternative Overlap

All twenty-two of the alternative spiritualists I interviewed indicated that in some ways there were no sharp distinctions between being part of the mainstream and part of countercultural spirituality. Despite frequent emphasis on being "different" from the mainstream, there was talk of shared problems or conditions that no human being could escape. However, as an alternative spiritualist one was depicted sensitive to these situations — often more so than other types of persons. Thus, interviewees appeared to embrace an overriding commonalty amongst all persons, while still promoting countercultural spirituality.

For Maria, the word "community" meant "the whole planet, and then community is all life even beyond the planet." She elaborated on some of these sentiments when giving her opinion of mainstream society:

It's in dire need of — of a lot of revaluation, reconstruction and reimagining. It's just — mainstream society is just completely disillusioned. But at the same token, we can't escape it. We are all mainstream society, so it's — you gotta be real inclusive and you have to integrate. You can't stand on the outside of mainstream and, "Change, change, change, we hate you." You've got to integrate and you've gotta realize that — I had somebody say to me, "Oh, those New Agers, nah-nah-nah-nah, you know, and blah," and I said, "You know, unfortunately, we're all in this together, you know, so can't really — you know, it's an illusion to think the New Agers are over there and you're over here."

Maria spoke to the need for all people to stop thinking they are different or better than others, and she expressed this in a way that nonetheless asserted herself as an alternative spiritualist with important insights that those around her did not necessarily possess. The strain between being mainstream and spiritual was addressed in a way that still featured a fundamentally spiritual outlook.

When asked if he met other people who shared his beliefs, Ralph answered:

Yeah, lots of people [share my beliefs], you know, not necessarily — they don't have to be Rainbow People but you know, you could share some of my beliefs with me, and you know, it's — you know, even my parents share some of the same beliefs with me, and I'm sure I've derived some of my beliefs from them. And, um, I'd say [the] majority of my friends — same — share the same beliefs with me and the majority of my friends, some of them don't share the same beliefs with me. But that's not going to stop us from being friends.

Without giving any indication of abandoning or compromising his beliefs, Ralph conceptualized the possibility of virtually anyone having relevance to his belief system. In fact, he acknowledged that he might well have acquired some of his beliefs from persons who were not countercultural spiritualists. Strains between being or not being an alternative spiritualist (i.e., a "Rainbow" person[1]) were dealt while still promoting his spiritual identity.

Criticism in Perspective

Even though each person I interviewed had criticisms toward mainstream society, each of the twenty-two people also made remarks that indicated that this criticism was not absolute — that the speaker was aware of his or her inevitable connections to the mainstream, and so launched his or her criticism with an awareness of this.

After criticizing mainstream society for its superficiality and tools for making people "numb," Flora went on to say:

I use those things, too, and I need them. And I recognize that when I'm really tired and I've been doing a lot of work that sometimes I just want to sit in front of the TV and watch a movie and relax and chill out that way, and that's okay. But I see the way that our culture is set up as attempting to keep people in specific forms and specific roles that aren't necessarily — that are not in my opinion healthy, and I don't like that. However, I also realize that, you know, I'm born into this world, and this is my culture and this is my society whether I like it or not. And my challenge is to learn to be the being that I am in an integrated way with this culture and this society.

Accepting of her participation in mainstream pursuits, Flora nonetheless indicated that much of the mainstream world was not "healthy" in her opinion. But she tempered this admitted opinion (as opposed to irrefutable fact) by also stating that she was part of this world. Still, a countercultural spiritual perspective dominated the articulation of the strain between mainstream and alternative ways of living.

The following was Marcie's vision of mainstream society:

I think people are basically all the same. Mainstream, alternative, I think they're really pretty much basically the same. I think people are basically good people who have good intentions, and if given the choice they will do what they think's right. I think most people are like that. I don't harbor any — although I wish — I wish they would question things a little bit more than they do. They take things for granted. I think mainstream society — and I include the alternative people in that — I wish they wouldn't be so selfish and narcissistic.

Criticisms were launched, but Marcie was hardly absolutist in the way she phrased them, and she embraced a certain commonalty amongst all people at the same time. Interestingly, Marcie included countercultural spiritualists in her criticism of people being overly "selfish and narcissistic." Yet, even though she asserted that all people were essentially alike, she presented herself as one who had spiritual insights into this overriding condition. The mainstream/alternative strain was discussed in a way that permitted the spiritual perspective to be advanced.

ACCEPTANCE OF MAINLINE RELIGION

Overlap with Alternative Spirituality

Despite the strain between mainline religions and alternative spirituality — and the allegedly negative experiences many interviewees claimed to have had within mainline religions — all of the people I interviewed (with the exception of Badger) gave at least some indication that mainline religions could be worthwhile.[2] In fact, seventeen of the people I interviewed told anecdotes concerning some sort of direct, interactive and positive connection with mainline religions that did not seem to stand in contradiction to their countercultural beliefs. Yet in these instances, the alternative spiritual viewpoint still dominated. For example, consider the following information from Larry:

I started having very detailed conversations with my parents about spirituality. The first time, I think, was about *The Book of John* with my father. I'm most attuned with the religious concepts of my father, because he — when he talks to me about these things, he gets to talk about things that he can't talk about as a parish priest. . . . One other way I've come back in contact with the Christian church is that I directed a production of *Godspell*, and this is where it all sort of came together for me . . . I incorporated Pagan elements. I used the "spiral dance" in there. And I changed the language so that it was more — so that it wasn't as specific, so that it wasn't, uh, as, uh, gender-biased, and it wasn't as, uh, religious-based.

While elements of Christianity were being realigned within Larry's countercultural spiritual framework, they nonetheless were being accepted as part of it. The strain between mainline religion and alternative spirituality was addressed, but in a manner that indicated preference for countercultural spirituality — even as mainline religion was viewed as having value.

Laurel conveyed the following story:

I had a neat experience this morning, too, where one of my next door neighbors, um, this [age] kid is very fundamentalist Christian, and we have a lot of fun hammering at each other. But you know, he started out trying to, oh, get — save my soul, you know [laughter]. And I'll rib him. And he didn't want to hear what astrological sign he was, but I — you know, I told him, it means you're a real leader, and it means you're charming and sociable and he — he started wanting to know and he's really interested in it, and then he started talking to me about it. And, um, I'm interested in his view of Christianity. I think Christianity is a basically beautiful, healing religion, it just hasn't been practiced, it got screwed up.

Laurel related that she had an enjoyable friendship with a conservative Christian. She even indicated approbation for Christianity at large. She also indicated that it had gotten "screwed up," whereby the strain between the two ways of believing was viewed through the overriding lens of alternative spirituality.

Ideologically Empathetic

Besides conveying actual positive experiences with mainline religions, there were other comments made that simply expressed positive sentiments or empathy for mainline religions. Once again, these comments were made within an overriding ideological framework of countercultural spirituality. Everyone I interviewed except Badger made a statement to this effect. Reflecting on the state of the American church, Iris said:

I think that the church in America provides a very important social place. That it has become the tribe of today's society, and it has become the place where we take our kids to learn values. They're not going to get it in school, so I feel that complete rejection of church is — is for many people rejection of a community. You know, I feel — I feel very much for the people who are raising kids without any sort of tribe at all, or any sort of way to learn things like this. You know, if I hadn't thought of God so much as a little kid, maybe I wouldn't be so spiritual now.

The American church was viewed by Iris as providing at least some sense of community and values, and she understood why people would find this important. But this opinion was voiced from an alternative spiritual perspective, in which people were viewed as trying to find a "tribe" to belong to. Her early training in conservative Christianity contributed to her current spiritual worldview, but not in a proactive way; it planted a proverbial seed, but she grew away from it. Positive remarks about organized religions were addressed in the course of reckoning with the strain with countercultural spirituality, but Iris clearly remained loyal to the latter worldview.

While Anthony did not talk about his spirituality overlapping with mainline religions per se, he did offer the following comments on mainline religions:

I think that they teach very good things. I think that they should be listened to more. I think that they are every bit as important as the more esoteric subjects. One thing is in [place of residence] voodoo is close to being a mainline religion. I was "Teacher of the Year" last year and the reason I was — part of it — was because when I was introduced to the PTA and everything, [they said] I was "Teacher or the Year" who wrote a book on voodoo. You know, that that is — is a part of the cultural expression. I think that one thing that needs to happen — the — the cult — the culture — it would be good if the culture became a little more cosmopolitan, and saw the value in different traditions.

Even as Anthony maintained that mainline religions were as significant as "esoteric" spiritual pursuits, he simultaneously criticized the ethnocentrism of the mainstream. Yet he indicated that these more "esoteric" pursuits were not about to be abandoned on his part, as evidenced by the positive impact that his pursuit of voodoo has had in his everyday life. Once again, the strain between organized religion and alternative spirituality was dealt within a manner that reflected approval of the former, while still promoting the latter.

Acknowledgment of Change

In fourteen of the interviews, there were comments to the effect that mainline religions were changing in positive directions — that is to say, becoming more ritualistically and ideologically aligned with countercultural spirituality. Therefore, while these comments cast mainline religions in a favorable light, so doing was based on alternative spiritual standards. Once again, the ideological strain at hand promoted countercultural spirituality.

Sylvia was fond enough of the Protestantism of her childhood to consider becoming an ordained minister. Ultimately, she found its conceptualizations too limiting (though not necessarily of no value), and set out along a different, more diversified path. Apropos of this, she had the following to say about mainline religions:

They've been changing. They've had to change. One of the things they discovered is a lot of people were going into, um, as they say, the occult. Which means they — that whole shebang — as opposed to New Age, because that's a specific term now, so I'm using the occult to mean New Age, Pagans, Hindus, Buddhists, the whole bit. Um, the non-mainstream stuff. Um, they discovered that people were just leaving, because church was boring. They had taken all the ecstasy, all of the passion out of it, and it was routine, rote kind of thing. Um, which is not how it was. In the early part of our country, Catholics still believed in daily miracles, that miracles could happen, and I think mainstream religion kinda got away from all that. I'm not really sure how that happened, I'm not — I don't have a historical background on Christianity. Um, but I think they're beginning to let that sort of thing back in.

Sylvia could praise mainline religions to the extent that they have been able to engage in such pursuits in the past or present — to the extent that they can meet her standards as an alternative spiritualist. In the strain between the two domains, countercultural spirituality was promoted foremost.

Though Jack did not speak favorably about his early experiences with Catholicism, he did make the following allowance:

It's getting better, I think. Catholicism is getting better, I think. I've heard of a few Catholic priests who do believe in reincarnation. And, uh, the Wiccan religions, I think, are getting more famous, so that's also good. And, um, I also see other religions getting more fame, like Hindu religions and all that, and — and more cultural richness in America. And that's kind of good. Especially

Native Americans' [religion]. I think they're really doing well so far, so it's gotten hold, I think.

Jack's spiritual eclecticism favors acceptance of diverse religious claims, whereby Catholicism was getting "better" because some priests might be becoming accepting of reincarnation. And society at large similarly met with his approval for embracing more diverse spiritual claims. His alternative spiritual viewpoint dominated the manner in which he dealt with the strain between Christianity and countercultural spirituality.

LIMITATIONS OF ALTERNATIVE SPIRITUAL IDENTITY

General Ideological Limitations

Limitations of self are often taken for granted by alternative spiritualists. But these limitations are used as a means for deeper self-reflection, and for keeping one's quest for spiritual understanding lively and engaging. Countercultural spiritualists are not beyond expressing hedonistic desires, and when interacting, the sound of laughter is hardly uncommon. However, as the popular literature suggests (and as both the interviews and my personal experience would verify), these are fundamentally serious, introspective people. They constantly seek out newer and deeper understandings of both their personal destiny and the nature of the world around them, and are ever-busy honing their ability to find spiritual meaning in all things. [3]New thoughts and information are almost continually being scrutinized and sorted through. Whether it be a major world event, a childhood trauma, or even a seeming tendency to always get stuck at the red light, experience is carefully examined for spiritual implications.

Hence, potential threats to one's alternative spiritual identity can be subsumed within one's overriding spiritual viewpoint. Doubts, contradictions or dilemmas can seem relatively unimportant when compared with the time and thought one had already invested in these pursuits. And perhaps solution for these potential limitations was at hand, if one continued to delve deeply into the self. Each person I interviewed made some sort of statement to this effect.

Edward talked about what he called "inner" versus "outer" ways of knowing, explaining the difference as follows:

Inner knowing is a certainty that is not backed up by logic. A lot of people call that "intuition," but I see intuition as a kind of pole-vaulting that's really fast, but it doesn't necessarily need a whole lot of data to work with. Inner knowing is just a certainty. This applies to other things in your life, and if you choose to perceive it consciously, it can become a faculty that's real handy for a lot of things. And I use that. I'm not as — as skilled with it as I will be in five years, but I'm getting there. Essentially with my — what I use inner knowing for is to test whether my hypothesis is right about the nature of perception, because instrumentation hasn't been developed yet to look at it. And I'm working on developing it, since not much of the scientific community will [laughter].

While Edward readily admitted to not having fully articulated answers for the many spiritual concerns that interested him, he also affirmed confidence that he would. Moreover, he launched a critique at the mainstream scientific community, which he viewed as not even attempting to take on these important issues.

Here is a statement from Alex:

Sometimes I get in arguments with one of my friends, 'cause he's really skeptical about any sort of like faith or religion, and we get in these huge discussions, and it's really hard to like, I don't know — having to defend myself because I'm not always that, you know — in pressure situations I'm not the best at being clear about what I'm talking about. And so the skeptic takes over and is like, "Well, you know, maybe he's right, maybe you are just, you know, living this lie or something." [Laughter.] But then I think, "Okay, is that really true?" And then I think of all the, you know, all the times that — all the people I know because of this, and all the really intense feelings thoughts I've had before because of, you know, this sort of faith that I have. And that usually, you know, like intuitively I'm like, "No, that's right, that's good." I'm not hurting anyone, you know, it's no different than anything else, any other religion, you know, and actually it's not nearly as dogmatic as probably most.

Despite admitting to skepticism, in general Alex felt she was gaining both socially and introspectively for having pursued countercultural spirituality. In addressing the strain between believing and not believing, she also noted that her belief system was at least not "dogmatic" like other kinds were. In sum, she ultimately favored alternative spirituality despite her honest confrontation with her doubts.

Unresolved Ideological Issues

In fifteen different interviews, there was mention of an unresolved dilemma that was challenging the individual's spiritual outlook. But the situation was not causing the interviewee to abandon her/his spirituality, as one had faith that an answer would be forthcoming. In the meantime, the issue was being considered within a countercultural framework. For example, here is how Arthur explained his efforts to spiritually reckon with getting divorced from a woman whom he felt the "Sumerian Babylonian Goddess of Ishtar" had brought into his life:

For me, that was a real — almost a violation of an agreement that I had with myself and with the universe. You know, with this Goddess. And you know, I said, "Hey, I gave you my part of the deal, where's my part coming back?" And, uh, it's been an interesting transition dealing with that, dealing with what can be interpreted as a betrayal by the universe. Uh, uh, to a large extent, I've gone hot and cold on it. Um, I've, you know [name] is a wonderful, and, uh, [child's name has] changed my life in many, many ways — many — some good, some not so good [laughter]. You know, in general, let's say an experience well worth it himself. And it's not to say I didn't learn a lot with [ex-wife's name]. I certainly did. I learned a lot about what myself, I learned a lot about life. Um, I guess in a sense my way of dealing with it, is that I'm still waiting. I'm saying, "Okay, that wasn't it. What are you going to come up with next?" Because the universe has been throwing a hell of a lot of stuff at me lately.

Arthur freely admitted to experiencing unpleasant surprises and doubts in his life, but he still discussed these matters in an alternative spiritual frame of reference. He did not say, for example, "Now I don't believe there was a Goddess," or "Maybe life is random coincidence." Instead, he stated that the "universe" had been challenging him, and that it seemed like the Goddess had betrayed him, and he anticipated some form of spiritual resolution. Strain between his spiritual ideals and mundane reality was addressed, while still promoting his spiritual belief system.

Unresolved spiritual issues did not have to concern major life events. For example, in the midst of explaining his general spiritual beliefs and experiences, Eli suddenly discussed the following:

A dissonance in my worldview that I haven't resolved — and since it doesn't trouble me lately I probably am not going to bother, ha! But you know I have a sacral worldview, everything that is is holy because it is, the very fact that it exists makes things holy. At the same time, I go through — from time to time — a — a lot of trouble to erect sacred — sacred space, erect a temple. And there's an extreme illogic in that, in that I think that I'm already standing on sacred ground — ground and scared space. Why do I go through all this trouble to erect more sacred space? Uh, I don't have an answer for that.

Without prompting from me, Eli frankly talked about what he perceived to be dissonant in his spiritual worldview. He even poked gentle fun at himself in presenting an additional strain in his striving not to let this bother him verses the inevitability that it would (i.e., "ha!"). In the meantime, Eli gave no indication of abandoning spirituality for this apparent contradiction. Indeed, the matter itself involves deeply held spiritual beliefs, whereby his countercultural spiritual frame of reference dominates and is promoted in his presentation of the strain.

Limitations of Self

Other comments in the interviews indicated not so much the seeking of a theoretical solution as simply accepting one's limitations as a human being. However, acknowledgment of these shortcomings did not necessarily diminish

one's commitment to alternative spirituality. Striving to deal with one's shortcomings could seem spiritual unto itself, given the strong emphasis on self-
reflection in countercultural spirituality. Once again the alternative spiritual
agenda was promoted in addressing the strain at hand — in this instance,
between one's desired and perceived actual self. With the exception of Badger,
all of the people I interviewed made some sort of remark concerning recognition of personal shortcomings. For example, Clarissa conveyed the following:

I have like the heart and mind battles, kind of like I — I can always feel it if
I'm trying to make a decision, like my — like they'll be — there's always like
two voices that I'm hearing, like one is from my heart, one is from my head.

When I asked her how she handles these moments, she replied:

Sometimes I freak out [laughter]. I mean, I'm definitely — you know, I
have a long way to go, lots to learn. And I feel like one of the biggest steps is
being aware of these things. But I don't have some magical solution when I
have these battles. Sometimes I just totally freak out and don't know what to do
and get all upset [laughter].

While admitting to her inability to do much besides "freak out" at times,
Clarissa also saw this situation in terms of seeing just how far she had to go in
her spiritual development, and that she was making important progress simply
by being aware of the situation. The strain was addressed within an overriding
spiritual framework.

When Anthony was asked if he encountered challenges to his spiritual
beliefs in his daily life, he laughed and replied:

Every day. Every — absolutely every day. Um, okay — there is — part of
my spiritual beliefs is that the importance of my existence is to be — is to be
compassionate, to show compassion toward others. . . . All I have to do is get
out on the road, you know, and get in the car, and at that point [my] beliefs are
challenged and I either come through or I don't. The thing that's important
now is I realize when I come through, and I realize when I don't come through.
I realize when I exercise compassion and I don't make excuses for when I don't.
Or if I do make excuses, I admit that I'm making excuses for myself. . . . Usually,
about fifty percent of the time, about fifty percent of the day, there will be some
sort of magical working.

Anthony maintained his spiritual beliefs despite the fact that only about
half the time did he feel he lived up to his ideals. But he felt that becoming
more aware of this distinction in and of itself indicated spiritual growth. In
sum, he accepted his self-limitations in such a way as to still promote countercultural spirituality.

"Unspiritual" Self

Even though interviewees largely concentrated on their identity as alternative spiritualists, in eighteen cases there was also salient discussion of what might be called one's mundane or "unspiritual" self. Technically, countercultural spiritualists view everyone and everything as sacred, but since no one is absolutely committed to any one ideology, there were moments in the interviews when people framed their sense of self in more mundane terms. Yet in these cases, an overriding spiritual frame of reference remained apparent.

Marcie was one of the more well-known alternative spiritualists within the informal network of persons that I studied; the type of individual whom "everyone knew." I might have guessed that she would be more firmly convinced of her spiritual beliefs than many of the people I interviewed. However, she was possibly the most skeptical. I asked her why she remained so highly visible a participant in countercultural spiritual activities if she had so many doubts about them:

I'm a dyed-in-the-wool romantic, obviously. I really want this stuff, a lot of it, to be true. I would really want it to be true that we're just not a bunch of little ants crawling around on the surface of the earth. Or you know — I would like us to do something more than just be parasites. I want something more to be there. I want — I want me and the world to achieve greater things. It's a drive. And so I think that's probably Number One. And, um, why do I continue doing this? Because I want to figure out what — I just — I just want to know — I just want to know what — why people believe in things. I have this real interest in why people believe in things. Maybe if I can figure out that [laughter], I can figure out the rest.

Marcie described herself as a "romantic," and someone who was curious to know "why people believe in things." Thus, she was admitting to aspects of self not contained within her alternative spiritual identity per se; people who were not countercultural spiritualists might be intellectually curious or "romantic." Still, she *wanted to* believe there was spiritual aspect to life, and pointed to this belief as highly desirable, for it would give her a sense of meaning in life beyond the purely mundane. So she promoted countercultural spirituality, despite her skepticism.

Steven experienced a health crisis for an extended period of time. I asked him what he would say on a television talk show if asked why he did not use his magical skills to cure himself. This was his response:

When they ask you why you can't heal yourself of any given illness — well, generally, when you're sick, you're too miserable, and you just don't have enough concentration. People just don't seem to understand that point. . . .

There were a couple of times when my interest in magic was pretty much the only thing that kept me going. And I also don't think I really would have been able to muster much ambition, much focusing on anything — like my education — otherwise. [I probed for an example] Well, like I say, the year I spent [with health problems], one of the things I was doing was reading everything on magic I could get my hands on. And no, it was not the sort of case where I was looking for a particular spell that would effect a cure. It was beyond that, because I was researching the subject for its own sake, because it interested me.

Steven stated that his interest in magic did not magically cure his condition, but it did provide him with other resources. His pursuit of these activities was not always to advance spiritually as such. Like anyone else, he also sought something to engage his interest. Steven also frankly stated that he felt "too miserable" to effect much spiritual power — he was a patient needing recuperation, and not exclusively an alternative spiritualist per se. Still, while discussing the strain between the reality of illness and spiritual ideals, he strongly promoted his commitment to countercultural spirituality.

LIMITATIONS OF ALTERNATIVE SPIRITUALITY

Lastly — though hardly of least significance — the individuals I studied were not beyond finding problems, contradictions, or limitations within the alternative spiritual movement. Once again, recognition of these imperfections does not necessarily lead to an abandonment of one's spiritual belief system. Since the ultimate authority for what is right for the self is the self, and since activities are but loosely structured at best, it was fairly simple to extricate oneself from a particular activity, group, or individual that one found fault with. Also, realizing these instances of inconsistency or contradiction outside the self could be cause for self-reflection, or create a sense that one was advancing spiritually for these insights that others were not necessarily having.

No one I interviewed made an explicit claim that countercultural spirituality existed in some rarefied state of perfection. In fact, eighteen persons made explicit mention of some form of disagreement or conflict with some aspect of the alternative spiritual milieu.[4] Comments concerning the strain between what others were thinking or doing versus one's personal insights nonetheless served to fundamentally promote alternative spirituality.

Alternative Dogma

The people I interviewed so intensely sought a flight away from group dogma that often they were sensitive to it even when it appeared in alternative spirituality. Fourteen interviews made explicit comments to this effect. For example, consider the words of Gypsy, in describing how she came to develop her own form of spirituality:

A lot of the stuff that I was reading was a little bit more, uh, simplistically Wiccan-based. You know: casting circles, calling forth elements, making an intent, raising the kind of power, bringing it down, grounding, closing the circle and calling — you know, thanking the elements. So I was like, well, it seemed awfully simplistic, and it didn't really work for me very well. I — I respected it, but it didn't work for me. So I kept looking for things that worked. And that was one of the things this woman [who gave Gypsy spiritual counsel] had mentioned was that you should — your spirituality is whatever works for you. You know, just because someone else has like for example, [an organization's] massive rituals and things like that — that works for them, it doesn't work for me. I'm not very good with coordinated rituals. So I started looking more and more into what I was doing.

In discussing spiritual strain between modes of alternative spiritual practices, alternative spirituality was still being promoted. Her criticism was not toward countercultural spirituality at large, only in the way some people approached it. Also, Gypsy maintained the overriding alternative spiritual ideology that if something worked for others, that was fine for them, though not necessarily for herself.

Eli was trained in what he called "high magic," but generally preferred not to use it:

I don't like it because you focus extremely intensely on one thing. It's reductionist. Indivisible particles, you know — you pull out this angel and put it on the slide and you look at it. And that's really good if you've gone out to string them all back together, but life isn't cut like that, and [better] witchcraft focuses on complexes of entities rather than on discreet entities.

Eli's comments indicated that just as in other belief systems, there were disagreements about how to practice magic. In his view, some people practiced a highly-routinized form that was too simplistic for addressing the full aspect of life experience. Yet he did not suggest that countercultural spirituality was not worth pursuing, only that some people tended to be "reductionist" in the way they approached it.

Becoming a Religion

In twelve interviews, the issue of alternative spirituality becoming dogmatic was discussed even more explicitly: in terms of alternative spirituality becoming so codified that it was becoming a religion, the very thing allegedly it was not supposed to be.

Jesse described his eventual disenchantment with a fairly organized countercultural spiritual movement as follows:

I thought that people were throwing out the baby with the bath water. And um, by negating other religions in order to hold their religion up — in other words, their spirituality was now becoming a religion. Yep, and I didn't like that.

High spiritual ideals were being promoted even as Jesse made apparent his dislike for the group's metamorphosis into a kind of "religion" for its dogma and limitations.

Badger was extremely outspoken — one might almost say zealous — in his strong preference for communally-oriented, environmentally-friendly country life. Still, at one point during the interview, he made the following observation:

When you're out in the country it just seems like it breeds its own form of insanity, and people get real imbalanced from being isolated a lot of times. Like in [place] we just see limited numbers of people and we don't get that much mix or variety, and — and it needs to kind of equal out. . . . There's like a loose kind of, um, underground of people in [place] that have different earth-based spirituality[ies], and I'm wondering how their kids are going to turn out. 'Cause like they'll see us get together on, um, solstice and different, you know — a lot of times different, uh, moon phases. You know, people get together, and I'm kind of wondering what — you know, I see a lot them getting real bored with the things we're doing, and I'm wondering what its going to evolve to. Because the [Catholic] mass is so repetitious, and a lot of times we had people that I don't think were really inspired saying what they were saying. I think they were just kind of there, you know, they really — I think they were kind of there against their will, or they weren't really doing what they were really inspired to do. Or they didn't inspire me. They were inspired, but they weren't inspiring me.

Badger wondered whether what he and his peers viewed as "spiritual" was becoming its own form of limitation. In fact, he speculated as to whether or not certain individuals were finding this "spirituality" to be so much force of habit — whether it was paralleling his own unhappy experience with Catholicism. (Interestingly, he also was careful to state that Catholicism was not necessarily uninspired, but that it did not inspire him. As an alternative spiritualist, he wanted to avoid any dogma on his own part.) Still, while Badger felt the lifestyle he was a part of needed to "equal out," he gave no indication of discontinuing involvement with it. The very fact that he was concerned with the group finding more balance spoke to an overriding allegiance to countercultural spiritual ideals.

Ideology Versus Reality

Besides criticisms involving drifts toward dogma, there were other disparaging remarks toward the alternative spiritual community made during interviews. Such comments concerned a general sense of a strain between the ultimate purpose of countercultural spirituality verses how it might be enacted given human limitations. These remarks occurred in fourteen interviews.

Flora conveyed the following experience:

I'd worked a lot with the medicine cards. I used to sit in [a] park and read people's medicine cards for them. Um, till I found out that people really didn't wanna know what their lessons were, and decided it was really a waste of my time [laughter]. So most people, not all people, but in general people just want an interesting experience. They don't really want to know what's happening with their lives. And that's what I would always tell them, and they didn't like it a whole lot. Or they liked it but they could never deal with it, or whatever.

"Medicine cards" (a form of divination based on Native American wisdom) allegedly were utilized to inform the seeker of his or her present state of affairs. However, in Flora's estimation, many people were using her readings of the cards for more mundane purposes. While ultimately she stopped offering these readings, Flora did not indicate that there were problems with the explanatory power of the actual cards, or that alternative spirituality was not valid. Being spiritual ideally meant striving to become more honest and self-aware, even as in Flora's view, most people could not manage to do so very well.

Given the emphasis in countercultural spirituality on saving the earth, perhaps the single most devastating criticism concerning alternative spiritual ideals versus reality was voiced by Melanie. She was referring to a large-scale event that many different kinds of people attended. Nonetheless, this was what she had to say:

I went to [a large-scale event] last year, and the whole thing was about, you know, community and staying together and healing the earth. And when everybody left, it was no longer a field of grass. It was a field of trash. Granted, I was in [a city], but I don't think it would have been any different anyplace else. I don't really think that people like to look at themselves because they'd be scared to see what's really there. And I don't like — I want to be able to love myself and like myself and say that I've done my part, and be as honest with myself and other people as possible. And get over — conquer my fears so that I don't have to come back next time.

Melanie expressed little faith that most people could change enough to help make the world a better place. At the same time, she gave no indication of abandoning her own ideals to heal the earth or find community; the overriding alternative spiritual values were good ones, even though most people could not live up to them. In Melanie's view spirituality was helping her to become better able to look at herself; that was what mattered the most. Indeed, she ultimately affirmed her belief in reincarnation and her own high spiritual goals.

CONCLUSION

The people I interviewed maintained spiritual beliefs that some would find difficult to accept, but this did not mean that the interviewees necessarily were "unrealistic" people. In fact, they frequently discussed what they perceived to be personal or community-level limitations regarding what could realistically be accomplished by the countercultural spiritual movement. Yet even when they admitted to these limitations, they often did so in ways that upheld and promoted their overriding spirituality. Disparaging remarks were framed within an alternative spiritual context.

As with any other form of group or community, some people were more committed than others, or had insights or criticisms that other people in the group did not share. But again, as with other kinds of groups, seeing limitations to what one could accomplish did not automatically mean that one would no longer try. Moreover, there were patterns of similarity across individuals that suggested still other sources of commonalty in the countercultural spiritual movement (as indicated in Table 5.1).

Table 5.1: **Frequencies of Ideological Limitations in Interviews**

Frequencies of Ideological Limitations in Interviews	N=22	Percent of Sample
ACCEPTANCE OF MAINSTREAM SOCIETY	22	100
Living in Mainstream	22	100
Mainstream and Alternative Overlap	22	100
Criticism in Perspective	22	100
ACCEPTANCE OF MAINLINE RELIGION	21	95
Overlap with Alternative Spirituality	17	77
Ideologically Empathic	21	95
Acknowledgment of Change	14	64

Frequencies of Ideological Limitations in Interviews	N=22	Percent of Sample
LIMITATIONS OF ALTERNATIVE SPIRITUAL IDENTITY	22	100
General Ideological Limitations	22	100
Unresolved Ideological Issues	15	68
Limitations of Self	21	95
"Unspiritual" Self	18	82
LIMITATIONS OF ALTERNATIVE SPIRITUALITY	18	82
Alternative Dogma	14	64
Becoming a Religion	12	55
Ideology Versus Reality	14	64

NOTES

1. "Rainbow people" refers to those who attend Rainbow gatherings, one of the more popular types of spiritual festivals that happen in various parts of the country throughout the year. "Rainbow" here is a metaphor for diversity; it is believed that all different types of people can be fundamentally part of the same "tribe" aimed at healing the earth (McGaa 1992). There are numerous other spiritual festivals held regularly that attract many of the same persons. Hence, "Rainbow person" can also suggest a more generic label: someone who does not literally attend Rainbow gathering but does attend (for example) the Starwood festival, or even small group activities — or at very least is in sympathy with many of these ideals.

2. If some readers might find these remarks patronizing, it is important to note that there are members of certain mainline religions who might not be nearly as charitable toward alternative spirituality in return.

3. Upon learning that they would be assigned an interview number for my records, several individuals expressed curiosity as to what the number would

be, and pondered the spiritual significance of this. Numerology is but one of many spiritual beliefs one encounters in alternative spiritual circles, and given that any information of potential spiritual merit, it was possible to look for mystical significance in one's interview number.

4. There were elements of intrigue — even gossip — within the loose social network I studied. As previously mentioned, the persons I interviewed either know each other or else know many of the same people. Some are at present or have been in the past intimately involved. When a couple split up, sometimes their friends took sides. In other instances, there had been disagreements over what to include in group activities, or who "really" did or did not understand the purpose of being spiritual (despite the ideological emphasis on self-auton-omy to decide these things). I was aware of several episodes across interviewees that were fodder for gossip, and in a few instances people even went on record discussing them. However, conveying such information was not my purpose.

6

Mythology as Ideology

In alternative spirituality, resolving of the alleged false dichotomy between matter and spirit sometimes takes the form of spiritualizing mundane life events. In this way, affairs involving "matter" can be conceptually unified with concerns of the "spirit." It could be said that this spiritualizing of the mundane is a form of mythology. Traditionally, "mythology" has been viewed as a body of stories aimed at explaining the human condition, and which is well-known to a particular culture or society. However, in a contemporary context, "mythology" can be said to involve stories or imagery known primarily to the self. Just as people feel free to pick and chose from various world religious traditions, they also feel relatively free to create a highly personalized mythos that has explanatory power only in regard to the self (Swartz 1985). There has been a body of popular literature on the topic of the spiritual and/or therapeutic importance of composing one's personalized mythology, and/or how to best go about doing so. As stated in a promotional flyer for a spiritual event I attended: "We create our mythology as we go along."

For my purposes, "mythology" can be said to serve the following purposes in a self-story: First, mythology presents life events in a coherent framework; second, that which is "mythic" contains elements of powerful idealization and perceived deep meaning beyond the mere recalling of events; third, one's mythologized interpretation can seem more compelling than other, less mythologized ways of describing the experience; fourth, it seeks to address symbolic strains within a situation (Travers 1975; Schneiderman 1981; Burke 1989; Griffin 1990).

Given that the mythologized account offers a coherent, idealized, and compelling means of dealing with symbolic strain, it could be argued that virtually any ideological declaration potentially contains elements of the mythic (e.g., political rhetoric). This would include any of the excerpts from interviews that have already been quoted. But for the sake of parsimony, I will limit dis-

cussion of the mythic in ideology to the following specific and highly salient
categories that appeared in the interviews.

MYTHOLOGY IN THE INTERVIEWS

Mundane Events Made Explicitly Mythic

Given the widespread belief in alternative spirituality that all aspects of life
are sacred, even the most mundane aspects of the life experience can be
endowed with elements of the mythic. Popular literature suggests numerous
examples. In an issue of *Science of Mind*, architect Anthony Lawlor discussed his
metaphysical approach to his vocation (Juline 1995:49). Among other comments, he explained how "The sacred in architecture is not out there but in
here, within us." In *Llewellyn's New Worlds of Mind and Spirit*, there were
thoughts on the subject of "familiars." Traditionally, these animal spirit "pres-
ences" have been said to be available only to highly trained pagans or witches;
however, the author pointed out that this is no longer the case: "If you have any
kind of pet in your home, one with whom you feel close, you already have a
familiar. Even if you don't have a pet, but are drawn to a certain kind of animal,
it may well be a sign you have an astral familiar. Familiars are around us all,
even in our daydreams and nightly dreams" (Conway 1995:10). And in the
June 1995 *Shambhala Sun*, there was an account of how what other people
would think of as a coffee break could be transformed into a "coffee meditation": "Sitting quietly with the coffee the caffeine has a chance to subtly perme-
ate and suffuse the body. . . . Rather gradually, sip by sip, you and the coffee
become one. Consciousness dawns. You are ready to make love with the day"
(Brown 1995:74).

In one form or another, all twenty-two of the persons I interviewed made
remarks that suggested a personalized mythologizing of the mundane. For
example, Laurel described her recent return to college as follows:

> To me, school is an intensely spiritual thing. It — well, it — all levels, um
> — it's wonderful being there, but I would not have said that two years ago if
> someone asked me. I go to school, life's the lesson, and now school is the place
> to be. So, um, and in — in school there's so much coming from the space of
> belief in past lives, or at least common ground that makes you feel like you've
> had a past life with somebody. You connect with people and that adds to the
> connection. I mentioned on the phone [when we were arranging the interview]
> things like in astronomy class — the different colors of the planets, the posi-
> tions of the planets, um, that can fit in with the chakras. And if you think that,
> okay, a planet that is in our solar system is going to have some effect on us here
> on earth, say [for example] Neptune, a huge, humungous blue monster out
> there. Blue is the throat chakra. That's creativity.

Stating that college was "intensely spiritual," Laurel proceeded to coherently illustrate how and why such was the case. Rational, secular information was reconceptualized as having deep, compelling, and idealized meaning — as did her social interactions at school. Being in college was not diminishing Laurel's sense of spirituality, but rather, was being subsumed within it. Her countercultural worldview was being promoted in the strain between rational and spiritual ways of knowing.

Sylvia related numerous experiences she has had in what is often called psychic healing. Yet she also related the following:

One of my more practical magics is, uh, I can find really cool stuff at garage sales and second hand stores. I have a zebra drum that couple of — I don't know, I guess it's about three foot across and it's made out of a zebra, the feet are zebra feet, and it's for eight to ten people across, and we can sit around and drum together. I got it at a garage sale for twenty-five dollars — okay, or maybe it was fifty, but still, it's like a seven or eight hundred dollar drum. So I — I am able to find — well, it does feel like that I am able to notice when the Divine is sending me something to one of these places. And I — that happens on a real regular basis. I've sort of gotten a name in the community for that. Um, so I find a lot of my magical objects that way, and take them all as gifts.

Simply having a good eye for a bargain at garage sale was not what Sylvia was describing; it was "magic"— something much deeper and potentially more interesting that served to symbolically unify the strain between the sacred and the mundane and affirm her spiritual identity. She found a drum, a popular spiritual tool among alternative spiritualists, and one that is at least partially made of "zebra," which can be suggestive of tribalism, animal spirit, or things of the earth.[1]

Mundane Events as Implicitly Mythic

Nineteen interviewees made comments that indicated that everyday events or activities were implicitly mythical. That is, everyday events were suggestive of deep, compelling idealized meanings that reckon with the strain between the sacred and the mundane. However, the speaker did not explicitly explain how or why such was the case. Given that all aspects of life were considered sacred, such declarations were not necessarily incoherent. But they did suggest that the countercultural spiritual ideology regarding the sacredness of all life was so deeply enmeshed within the speaker that no explanation seemed necessary.

Jesse (who elsewhere explained his complex spiritual belief system involving both ancient or otherworldly beings, as well as futuristic notions of science and space travel) was asked to describe his spiritual activities:

Taking care of my children — yeah, I take care of my kids a lot, I take — I don't — it's just integrated into everything that I do. I don't necessarily celebrate the season. A lot of people go, "It's the winter solstice, we gotta celebrate it."

And I go, "I am, I'm living it, I'm here." I'm pretty conscious of what's going on in the seasons, and the weather in nature, and try to tie my activities in conjunction with all of it, and try to make my life link to what's going on nature as much as I can.

Without elaborating how or why, daily life activities — the simple processes of living — were assigned a deep, mythic meaning that addressed the strain between concerns of matter versus spirit. A spiritual agenda was promoted as Jesse technically described his active interest in things such as his children or the weather, suggesting that viewing such pursuits as automatically spiritual was more compelling than not to do so.

When Anthony was asked what his spiritual journey meant to him in the present moment, he replied:

That I can sit here and be very calm during an interview, and be completely present at the interview, not thinking about a manuscript I went over, or who's coming here at six o'clock. That I can appreciate the feel of the table on my hands, and slight sound — sounds that the tape recorder makes, and the louder sound that the air conditioner makes, and the TV in the background. It — it's a matter of being present in the mystery of existence.

Given Anthony's deep immersion in voodoo and other practices, I might have predicted a response dense with spiritual terminologies. But in fact, virtually anyone could appreciate the feeling he described — while not necessarily understanding why it portended to "the mystery of existence." A strain between this "mystery" and being fully present in the material realm was addressed in a way to suggest deep, compelling mythic meaning, without explaining why.

Crisis Situations as Mythic

In eighteen different interviews, people discussed in mythic terms not just mundane events but a problem or crisis event. For example, Larry gave the following account of having once had an especially hectic semester as a student:

I was taking a language course at the time, and, uh, there was another course I was taking that was particularly demanding, and uh, confronting all that at the same time put me in a sort of crucible as far as my life was concerned. Uh, so that I was at that point of crisis, and then hitting, uh, a point of laughter, finding a point of humor in it, immediately allowed me to change the way I lived my life. Uh, it was a crucial point of transformation. It was sort of a gradual thing before that, but I look at that moment as a time in which I discovered my own life ethic of laughter, and seeing humor and trying to find the humor in painful situations, and dealing with comedy as a form — as a form of shamanic healing, uh, because comedy really does, uh, direct your body to it. Trying comedy is directed toward making your body hurt, and then laughter is the point of release at which you convert pain into bliss. Uh, so I mean I was able to articulate these terms as well, thanks to reading Joseph Campbell as part of my [studies and] part of my classical mythology work.

It is hardly uncommon for a college student to suffer anxiety for the demands of his course load. However, Larry described the situation as being a "crucible," a severe test or challenge that sets in motion a major "transformation" of self. Indeed, it was of a deeply spiritual nature, for the ultimate solution of finding humor in the situation was "a form of shamanic healing." Strains between mundane problems and spiritual ideals were mythologized, whereby the spiritual agenda was promoted for bringing a deep and compelling coherence into his life.

Maria spoke of some of her most serious life situations in a mythological context. She talked about the death of her husband as an important but troubling period in her spiritual journey:

The beginning of — of more of my cautious — cautious mystical and spiritual journey happened um, I think, oh, around the time of my daughter's birth, and also the time of her father's death. It was two years later, so the big impact was losing some — you know, losing someone like that close to me and having to have that person and to help that person through their passage, you know, of death. Like being with him when he died, being with him when he was dying. It just kind of made me just ask the big questions, so, um, I had some real, um, kind of channeled, um, experiences during — during his um, coma, where I was doing unusual praying. Unconscious things, you know, things that I wasn't thinking about were just coming. Passage kinds of hymns that I had learned about death, and, you know, going back into God's hands and I — see, I just started singing and praying those kinds of things during his coma, and I didn't . . . even know that um, he was going to die. I mean no one said, "He's gonna to die tomorrow." You know, it was like he was real bad, and we were just doin' all we could. But um, he did die the next morning, and um, it was really, um, you know, just like [an] unbelievable thing. And um, and then I suddenly — this little, you know, two-year-old, and um, not quite two-year-old daughter. And um, you know it was just the beginning of our partnership, I think, as far as not really being a nuclear family anymore but — but more of like okay, we're karmic partners now. And um, so over the years, over the next probably five years, I guess *my spiritual journey was a journey of doing things that were very unspiritual* [my italics]. . . . They forced me into other dir — other options. So it was real crazy period where I partied and I did a single's thing and um, you know — it was very empty and meaningless.

Like many people forced to deal with having a loved one in a coma, Maria sought to locate her experience within a spiritual context. Yet she did not simply pray for her husband, but did *"unusual* praying." As if some divine force was working through her, Maria seemed to know he was going to die shortly, although she had not been told that he would. As she tells it, this was not simply about the death of a loved one, or even of believing in God, but about profound psychic or spiritual messages allegedly being communicated to her. Maria and her daughter become not a single-parent family but "karmic partners." In short, her mythologized spiritual viewpoint dominated throughout her account of a stressful situation in which she was forced to reckon with the strain between human suffering and spiritual beneficence. That the mundane could be spiritually mythologized was perhaps most indicated by Maria's statement that for a time her spiritual journey consisted of doing unspiritual things.

Otherworldly Mythos Described as Literal

Twenty interviewees who described an encounter with the supernatural as a literal event.[2] No effort was made to prepare the listener by prefacing with words such as, "I know this is going to sound weird, but I swear this happened." Seldom did the speaker go on to offer "proof" that this was something "real" — and when he or she did, the "proof" was often quite mythical in itself.[3]

Like other comments made in interviews, these statements were essentially coherent. They served to advance alternative spirituality by suggesting a sense of something deeper or more compelling than immediate "reality." They also indicated efforts to address strain between the realms of matter and spirit.

Clarissa conveyed the following:

One experience basically changed my life. I was in — I was in the woods. I have — I have — most of the times when I feel most connected with like my spirituality and the source or anything is when I'm in the woods. Um, and one night I had this experience. It was the night of the full moon. Uh, I had contact with — with another like s — spirit being of some sort. Like, I don't know if you call them "fairies," I don't know what you'd call them. But I was in the woods, I — all of a sudden, I was just surrounded by all these blue like lights. They weren't lightning bugs, and they were coming toward us. They were definitely — I mean, you could sense that they were another being, but I really don't want to go into much detail about that. But I mean, after that, I — I was a totally different person, and I — I knew I always believed that there was a dif — a totally different realm, you know, The spirit realm. And, um, I had faith, you know, that it existed, but I had never really experienced it firsthand. And after that it was just, "Whoa, this is real, there is no doubt in my mind." And ever since then, I've been a totally different person, I guess.

Clarissa asserted that her most spiritual moments occurred in the woods, and coherently enough, that is where this episode transpired. An extremely mystical and dramatic encounter with the otherworldly was conveyed; given that Clarissa perceived it as real, it would not be difficult to see why it deepened her commitment to spiritual pursuits. Strains between matter and spirit were addressed by this alleged actual experience with the otherworldly, with the element of the mythic promoting the validity of countercultural spiritual claims.

Iris stated that she reached a point where she felt the fundamentalist God of her childhood "turned its back" on her. Later, I asked her if she meant this literally or figuratively. Given that she also made reference to concepts of spiritual oneness, I was expecting her to answer the latter, but instead she stated the following:

Literal. I literally mean that was like one of those "small still voice" experiences, where I said, "Okay, here is my prayer, I pray for this, I pray for some guidance. Look, I'm confused, I have this sexuality, and I know that it's a rightness and a goodness, and yet I'm being told that's a wrongness and an evilness, and that the things I'm doing with my sexuality are not socially acceptable. Where do I go with this?" And it was a very clear, very desperate even, prayer. You know, traditionally, in Christian traditions, it would be that, oh, you know, "Here, let me take you into my fold, let me forgive my prodigal child." It didn't happen that way at all. God said, "Oh, you found out. I give up." It was more like I could physically feel, you know, the entity I was speaking to — I could physically feel that entity turn on their [sic] back, and I sat and looked at their back.

In describing the strain between conflicting expectations regarding spirit and matter (i.e., sexuality), Iris made apparent her preference for alternative spirituality. The story served to make coherent and explicit — yet mythic — how and why she made a full break with the religion of her childhood.

Mythologizing Alternative Spiritual Self

Given the emphasis upon the self in alternative spirituality, it is not surprising that all twenty-two interviewees made statements indicating a mythologizing of one's spiritual self identity. In this way, one's countercultural spiritual self was depicted as being able to reckon with strains between the mundane and spiritual realms in a coherent, meaningful and compelling manner, whereby one's alternative spiritual self was presented as highly positive.

Spiritually Interconnected

Sixteen interviewees made comments that indicated a mythologized self that was profoundly interconnected with all aspects of life as a result of pursuing countercultural spirituality. For example, Eli was asked what his spirituality meant to him in the present moment:

It makes me feel superlatively isolated, yet inextricably tied to everyone and everything else [my italics]. It's like glittering stars, or separate stars that orbit a common point in space. We're like that. Our existence affects others. Their existence affects us. We are star individuals, and we learn the patterns, or — orbits or patterns of our actions, and feel this, and see how [we] link to others on the earth, in the earth, and see that even though we are a discreet entity we are still one with every other discreet entity.

The contemporary paradox between autonomy and a sense of community was well-illustrated by Eli's opening statement. He went on to give a poetical, idealized account of how he experienced this interconnectedness. Strains between individuality and belonging were addressed, and in so doing Eli presented a mythic and dramatic view of self. Taking him at his word, it would not be difficult to see why he finds his involvement in alternative spirituality to be important.

Edward was asked what he meant by the term, "greater self":

The greater self is kind of what a lot of people would call your soul. But essentially your greater self exists outside of the arena of space and time, and you're a projection of that into this reality. And everybody chooses to incarnate, and they choose to have a special task, if you will. Some people want to learn what love is about, so they are born into a situation of their choosing which will express love in many thousands of variations. I, for example, have chosen to understand perception, and I find myself in situations where I have to perceive in order to get through it, and it's a test by growth, by doing. And that's part of how we as humans evolve.

Edward dealt with a strain between individuality and interconnectedness with mythical explanations of why people are born into the lives they live. In the process, he promoted his countercultural spiritual identity, and the mystical destiny he perceived for himself.

Spiritually Empowered

In fifteen interviews, I find evidence of another approach to mythologizing the self: emphasizing not only an interconnectedness between the mundane and spirit world per se, but also an explicit sense that the self has become spiritually empowered or skillful for having pursued alternative spirituality.

In the course of explaining what her "dream rituals" consisted of, Gypsy noted the following:

Sometimes, it's um, I need — I'm interested in meeting another teacher, or I'm interested in meeting a spirit guide, to see what they have to say to me, like what do I need to know right now. Like I'm not even sure. Like I'm so confused right now I just need to push in the right direction. And, um, I'll put myself forth and try to send myself from a fairly mundane dream to something that's a little more detailed and elaborate and not that many familiar details, so that it's more so me in a completely different realm that I'm not really used to. And once I open myself up to that, generally I can open myself up to anything. And people are more willing — spirits and entities and — that to me are contained within me that are also contained within everything else, and it's just opening yourself up to different things.

Gypsy depicted herself as being able to accomplish life changes in a dream state, whereby she saw herself as spiritually empowered for having trained herself in this course of action. Strains between the mundane and spirit realms were addressed in a way that advanced Gypsy's claims about her spiritual self.

Arthur was asked how he dealt with challenges to his spiritual beliefs:

There are two Tarot cards. I don't know if you're familiar with the Tarot at all. One is the Fool, and the other is the Magician. And the Fool is the one who blindly goes out and accepts what the universe is gonna throw at him, okay? Uh, he is wise in the sense that he's been through it, um, but unwise in that he doesn't really know exactly what he's getting into, and he's just ready and willing to take whatever's handed to him. The Magician, on the other hand, is so connected with the workings of the universe that he's able to — to direct his will, and direct it in exactly the right way, to create manifestations. Um, I bounce back and forth between the two of them. Although I think many people would call me much more of a Fool than a Magician.

Arthur addressed strains in his life between mundane reality and spiritual idealism by symbolizing the former as the Fool, and the latter as the Magician — both of which he saw as aspects of himself. The Magician was the part of himself that was able to "create manifestations" — to work actual kinds of magic, according to Arthur. Arthur was able to present both a spiritually empowered self and a self that passively accepts the realities of fate while still promoting the more spiritual self.

Mythologizing Alternative Spiritual Community

Just how important a sense of community is to these individuals who simultaneously claim to possess a deep sense of autonomy was evidenced in comments made in all twenty-two interviews in which the countercultural spiritual community was endowed with an element of the mythic. In depicting this community as providing important and powerful experiences for dealing with strains between matter and spirit, the speaker was promoting alternative spirituality.

Specific Group Experiences

In fifteen cases, interviewees made mythic reference to the alternative spiritual community when describing a specific experience. For example, Mary Lou (who elsewhere stated that she did not align herself with an organized spiritual group) described the following event that occurred at a Native American ritual when asked to describe an especially significant experience:

There were two braves who were pierced and held back at the center tree, the holy tree, or whatever it's called. And, uh, they had red ribbons on their arms, you know, and they were praying and doing suffering to many, many reasons, and was symbolized with a — a red ribbon — red ribbon around the arms. It was like a band — it was like arm bands, and I sort of drifted off into this nappy little thing, you know, so warm. And I mean, it must not have been sleep but for like a minute or something, 'cause I'm very sensitive to the sun. I would have been burnt if I had been under it more than that. And then, I was under — I was in this dream state, and, uh, there was two huge birds that flew up above me and went hovering above me, just hover, just like on a — on a — on a air current, These bi — birds, like I don't know if they were hawks, or what it was. Just, you know, they were big birds, and they were just above me and circling and, you know, in my dream body, I saw that they were — they had the, uh, the had the — the red — red things on their legs, and I said, "Oh, wow, how'd you do that?". . . For me, it was just like a real blending of nature and human, you know, human religious experience, and so I woke up, 'cause you know, this was such a startling thing, and sorta like those little red things dissolved as I looked at them. They're uh — and then by that time, many other people were looking up in the sky, and saw these big bird hovering and then, uh, a general kind of slow, pleasing thing went over, and there's Indian medicine men and there's like all these people, these intensely religious Indian people who are going, "yeah." You know, they were — were agreeing that we all experienced the same sort of recognition, there was a messenger sent from nature, that we had actually communicated with nature, [and] become and accepted ourselves as being part of nature.

It was important to Mary Lou that she not only had this mystical experience that suggested a strain between the physical and spiritual realms, but also that other people there seemed to have a similar experience. The sense of significance one could obtain for participating in these sorts of spiritual rituals was self-evident, given Mary Lou's description.

Similarly, while Melanie stated more than once that she often preferred enacting rituals alone, she nonetheless described the following as a significant moment:

Actually there was this one [spiritual workshop] that only like six people showed up to. And [name] was running it, and we didn't know what we were going to do, and he said, "Okay, let's talk about men's and women's mysteries." There was one woman there that was um, she wasn't really prejudiced, but she was like, "You [men] can never know what it's like to be a woman." That was her argument, that was it. Everyone else that was there was very open, and it — it was so strange. It was like we were expanding our minds, and we all — like talking and playing off each other and it became like a big spiral, and I — I can remember three instances I'm like "Okay, don't interrupt me, I'm just like, this is just coming out," and they were so — they were realizations that in my mind were so profound. I have — within the two-and-a-half hour period of time I changed. Um, and I knew — I think that you change every moment, but when I walked out of there, and we were like, man, we were so drained. And it felt like that point where you can almost begin to grasp infinity, but your mind can't quite get there cause there's a block and it starts to hurt. That's what it felt like, and for two hours like there was something there that was getting closer and closer and bigger and I just — I really changed that night.

Technically, the group was addressing the popular topic of whether or not men and women were essentially different, and if so, how. But it was framed within the spiritual context of "mysteries," and for Melanie — and apparently the other people there — it was of an otherworldly profundity that resonated deeply within. It would seem that this was no ordinary gathering of people, in Melanie's view. Strains between understanding life within the earthly versus spiritual realm were dealt with, and her compelling spiritual testimony was advanced in the process.

Dyadic Experiences

Sixteen interviewees described having had an especially significant spiritual encounter with one other person in a countercultural context. For example, Alex described the following as being an especially significant spiritual experience:

Uh, I have really wonder — a really good friend, who, every time I see her, you know, we just — there's just really kind of a connection, and this is the same woman who told me — who went to [spiritual retreat], and we were really close, and some really — you know, usually just really good things happen to me when I'm around her. And I have another friend who — who, whenever I see him, you know, something really intense happens. And I'm being really vague here, because it — it's hard to be specific about things, just really good feelings like come about, and the timing is perfect. And um, a lot of it has been through people I've met more than experience in a lot of ways. I mean, besides being in the forest. I mean that, of course, is always really wonderful for me. But just people — people I share the same feeling — beliefs with that I've had amazing experiences with, usually keep me on the right track.

Simultaneous with Alex's desire (stated elsewhere) to practice a spirituality as free of dogma as possible was the importance she gave to what she felt to be a deep spiritual connection with these other people. A strain between her sense of solitude in the forest and her need for close ties with others was addressed. Alex asserted that she had had mythic experiences involving sudden shifts in life experience for making these connections — these were not depicted simply as pleasant times with friends.

A more explicitly mystical experience was described by Flora :

The next session I had with her, we had a [moment] of staring into each other's eyes, and the same thing happened to me that happens when I'm really present with people, and I don't know if it's flipping through their incarnations, different parts of energy or whatever. But we just sat and stared and were with each other, until we flipped back to the place where she looked like this Japanese master. And um, I don't really know exactly where we went, but I just knew that the fact that she was comfortable sitting there and doing that with me would make everything okay. That like the person was complete and able to deal with me. And that beginning therapy with this woman who [became] in some ways a spiritual teacher to me, really embarked me upon the leg of my journey that I'm on now.

Flora maintained that while "staring into each other's eyes" something of mythic proportions happened that she herself is not even certain how to define. Her encounters with this women were likened to a form of "therapy," but they were also of a mythic, spiritual nature. Interestingly, the time when Flora felt she was being most "present" was when this otherworldly state came upon her, whereby a strain between different modes of reality was indicated. Flora promoted alternative spirituality at large for being a milieu in which such experiences could transpire.

Drumming Circles as Mythic

Religious/spiritual rituals or otherworldly oriented exercises automatically transpire within an explicitly mythologized context. Simply by describing the event per se, one engages in mythology, without necessarily imbuing the description with one's *personalized* mythology. Thus, though there were plentiful stories from all interviewees regarding rituals, oracles, and so forth (some of which have been utilized elsewhere), I also was interested in how an activity that an outsider might not assume to be spiritual could be endowed with an individualized mythical meaning. Drumming circles provided an especially salient example. An outsider might have guessed that drumming simply provided pleasurable social interaction, but such was not the case: drumming was taken extremely seriously as a spiritual activity. However, since there were no universally agreed-upon rituals or pronouncements associated with it, the nature of this spiritual significance could vary from one individual to the next. In fact, sixteen interviewees described drumming circles in highly mythological terms that also were highly personalized. For example, Gypsy was asked what she meant by the word, "energy":

How about, for example, at a drum circle? Um, I try to always position myself at the drum circle so that I am in view of the drummers, and so that they can see the power of what they are producing does to my body. And, um, I do elemental dance, too. Like I'll call forth the north, call the, you know, like I can call forth the elements through the dance. You know, like if I'm, doing something for the north with earth, I'll be doing something low and deep and to the ground and like, working with energy low and deep. Work with something like fire, it's more like up and above. And generally, the drummers can feel when it's an elemental dance or when it's a power dance, and it's just — it's not just like listening to the music, but when they're getting into the spirit of the music, and through that, in my conversations with the drummers, that charges them. Every one — once in a while, I'll push towards them. Most of the time, when I dance, I'm in myself, and I send a definite core of energy through myself, and through the earth, and through the sky. So I feel it's like a definite polarity going through me. Sometime, I push that out, and um, give it to the drummers and put that out, and then when I put that out, it opens up an energy channel to me between the two of us, and I get the energy from them as they get — as I give it to them.

For Gypsy, dancing to the drums was an important spiritual pursuit that reckoned with strain between earth and sky — as well things like "above" and "below," or for that matter drummer and dancer. She felt she addressed these issues in a unifying manner that provided deep and compelling meaning for her. Gypsy promoted her countercultural spirituality while describing her experience.

Jerry was asked to comment on the word "synchronicity":

I think that point in magic where, for example, with a group of people who are drumming, and they have their intent in mind in that certain — when the drumming is everybody's heartbeat coming out in their drums. And it's just dancing there on the edge of reality. That's synchronicity.

Interestingly, though Jerry expressed considerable autonomy in regard to his approach to spirituality, he did not describe "synchronicity" in terms of a meaningful coincidence in his own life per se, but on a group level. For Jerry, it was the shared yet individualized experience of the drumming — the "coming out" of each person's heartbeat that provided meaningful coincidence. He saw this as a dance "on the edge of reality," whereby a symbolic strain between matter and spirit was addressed, and alternative spirituality was asserted as a significant pursuit.

Group Events as Mythic

Finally, seventeen interviewees described large-scale groups events as in and of themselves having a mythic power, beyond any sort of ritual or activity per se. For example, Ralph was asked to explain what "Rainbow gatherings" were:

Rainbow gatherings are like — it's like the Indians. Uh, I didn't know this awhile [ago], but the Indians prophesied that there would be a tribe of people when the earth was weeping and the things were getting really bad on the earth, here would be a tribe of people to come. You know, a great Indian leader saw this in a vision, and they would be called the Rainbow People, and these people would, uh, realize that, uh, we have to come back to the earth.

Ralph addressed strains between earth and spirit, and promoted Rainbow gatherings in the process, by discussing them in a compelling mythological context of prophecies, visions, and Native Americanism. He attempted to lend credence to these gatherings through these mythic elements, whereby "Rainbow People" — as opposed to mainstream society — could be seen as those who would heal the earth.

Clarissa described large-scale spiritual events and the informal network of persons who attend them as follows:

There's pretty much always one going on, there's one going on right now. Um, it's just kind of — I don't know if you want to call it like a peace and love gathering, where people get together and try to live — the goal, I guess, is to live in harmony with each other and with the earth, and it's kind of just like a traveling community. They move from forest to forest, and have gatherings, but — and just like share information and stuff. I — I met a lot of healers there, and just a lot of people who shared my beliefs, and that's how I learned a lot of stuff.

Clarissa appeared to view this community in highly mythical terms. She stated that these events not only dealt with strains between spirit and earth, but also that they were so abundant as to be "pretty much always" going on, and that they involved persons who traveled "from forest to forest" — almost like legendary creatures of the woodlands. She did not say, for example, "On weekends, when these people don't have to go to work, they drive on freeways to these events." The context is more meaningfully and compellingly mythical for Clarissa's promotion of countercultural spirituality.

CONCLUSION

Interviewees asserted that deep and compelling mythical meanings could be found in events, activities and/or one's personal destiny that outsiders would not have necessarily interpreted thusly. Seemingly contradictory strains regarding the sacred and the secular were frequently dealt with in ways that ultimately suggested preference for the alternative spiritual worldview. As indicated in Table 6.1, these comments also gave evidence of shared meanings and a sense of community across individuals.

Table 6.1: Frequencies of Mythology in Interviews

Frequencies of Mythology in Interviews	N=22	Percent of Sample
Mundane Events Made Explicitly Mythic	22	100
Mundane Events as Implicitly Mythic	19	86
Crisis Situation as Mythic	18	82
Otherworldly Mythos Described as Literal	20	91
MYTHOLOGIZING ALTERNATIVE SPIRITUAL SELF	22	100
Spiritually Interconnected	16	73
Spiritually Empowered	15	68
MYTHOLOGIZING ALTERNATIVE SPIRITUAL COMMUNITY	22	100
Specific Group Experience	15	68
Dyadic Experience	16	73
Drumming Circles as Mythic	16	73
Group Events as Mythic	17	77

Whether or not others would agree with any or all of the passages that have been quoted, they appeared to provide meaning and coherence as interviewees strove to live in a manner that addressed both matter and spirit. In the words of Marcie:

I would really like to believe that something happens to us after we die. I [don't] just want to die and that's it. I really would love to believe in reincarnation or moving on to a higher plane. Something — something other than just being dead and gone. That would really be wonderful to find that there was something beyond that.

NOTES

1. There is not universal agreement among alternative spiritualists regarding animal rights. Some might find it inhumane that an animal was used to make a drum, but others might feel that it is part of the primal natural cycles of the earth for humans to eat animal flesh or utilize animal skins, as exemplified by tribal cultures. In any event, given the emphasis on self-autonomy, people can be relatively unconstrained to decide these issues for themselves.

2. The remaining two interviewees spoke of having interest in otherworldly experiences, but did not explicitly convey any stories about having had any.

3. It should be noted that there are descriptions or enactments of encounters with otherworldly forces that are socially accepted. For example, people are not likely to ostracize the Catholic who believes in transubstantiation. Seemingly "normal," or "rational" people claim that they have seen or felt the presence of a ghost, were saved from a disaster by an angel, possessed by the devil, or believe their departed loved one periodically "visits" them.

Conclusion

SUMMARY

I sought to learn how alternative spiritualists reckoned with the contemporary strain between the desire for individual autonomy and a sense of shared community with others. To this end, I analyzed excerpts from in-depth interviews with twenty-two alternative spiritualists who considered themselves part of the same community yet did not necessarily share organizational ties or pursue the same spiritual belief systems, as this is the characteristic approach to countercultural spirituality. Based on my findings, it would appear that these people sometimes addressed issues of self and community the same way that any religious knowledge claim often is advanced: through the spoken word. People had ways of describing their beliefs and experiences that simultaneously suggested one's own worldview and a commonality with others.

In this way, I argued in Chapter 1 that alternative spirituality suggested a new form of social movement. In such movements, emphasis is placed not on strong organizational ties or explicit political agendas, but on advancing new communication codes that challenged existing social controls and dogma. When persons spoke as countercultural spiritualists, they were making declarations that fundamentally were ideological, in that they served to note and allegedly resolve a symbolic strain while simultaneously advancing one's interests as an alternative spiritualist. The common themes or ways of speaking across individuals indicated that there were forms of symbolic capital that these persons had in common, and which reflected ways of speaking in popular magazines, or at group activities.

Commonly, the strains addressed concern issues such as autonomy versus the need for community ties, as seen in Chapter 2, and/or the alleged false dualism in Western society concerning matter versus spirit. The latter strain often is addressed through issues such as science versus spirituality (Chapter 3), or other common dualisms such as earth versus sky as sacred, the female Goddess versus the male God, and darkness versus light (all seen in Chapter 4).

Even when discussing limitations of their ideology, selves, or the countercultural spiritual community, the persons I interviewed spoke in ways that served to promote alternative spirituality and diminish competing claims from mainstream society (as per Chapter 5). In fact, the interviewees frequently imbued aspects of self or community with an element of the mythic, whereby the claims being advanced might be viewed as all the more compelling or meaningful (Chapter 6).

While speaking about their personal experiences and beliefs, it would seem that interviewees very much framed their narratives around their identities as countercultural spiritualists, and were at least implicitly and often explicitly critical of the dominant, mainstream viewpoint in comparison. Even when referring to mundane experiences, mainstream knowledge claims, or more legitimized mainline religions, the alternative spiritual viewpoint dominated, whereby competing information claims were viewed as relatively positive or negative by countercultural spiritual standards.

Despite differences of beliefs or practices across individuals, often there was at least partial overlap insofar as what people believed or practiced. Additionally, the presence of common themes and shared critiques of the mainstream suggested commonalty and community. In sum, the alternative spiritualists in my sample seemed able to find ways of verbally expressing both a strong sense of individual autonomy and also maintain a desired sense of community.

DISCUSSION

In articulating the alleged differences between "religion" and "magic," Durkheim (1994:42) stated that while religion is that which is commonly shared, practiced and believed in by an identifiable group, "[m]agic is an entirely different matter. Granted, magic beliefs . . . are often widespread among broad strata of the population. . . . But they do not bind men who believe in them to one another and unite them into the same group, living the same life. . . . [T]here are no durable ties that make them members of a single moral body." According to Durkheim, religion needs and fosters group identity and interaction (or "church"), and so reinforces the collective conscience of a social order. Contrastingly, magic does not require a group setting (though it can take place in one), and represents an individual's desire to manipulate personal circumstance. Therefore, according to Durkheim, magic does not emerge from a collective effervescence that affirms social ties and values. Scholarship by authors such as Goode (1951), Titiev (1972), and Malinowski (1974) has offered similar conclusions.

However, these conceptual boundaries between "religion" and "magic" merit reconsideration when one considers the contemporary alternative spiritual community, which would not qualify as a "religion," and whose informal cluster of beliefs and practices often can be labeled "magic." It would appear that social networks that feature magic can promote a sense of community and shared values. Moreover, some of the people who participate in this networks state that a viable sense of community is exactly what they did *not* get from a more organized religion.

Furthermore, the enactment of "magic" or "religion" would not seem to cause one to be relatively isolated from or socially connected to others, nor does either practice necessarily emerge from a state of isolation or connection. Instead, it is important to consider large-scale social forces and institutions in which the magic or religion is being enacted. In a complex society, magic apparently can be utilized not only to manifest alleged change upon the self (as it has always been utilized to do). It can also be instrumental in articulating a collective social response against what Giddens (1994:6) refers to as "fundamentalism."

In this context, "fundamentalism means not necessarily religion but any social sphere that sees "tradition defended in the traditional way." Giddens writes, "The point about traditions is that you don't really have to justify them: they contain their own truth, a ritual truth, asserted as correct by the believer. In a globally cosmopolitan order, however, such a stance becomes dangerous, because essentially it is a refusal of dialogue." This "fundamentalist" refusal of dialogue, according to Giddens, precludes the necessary reflexivity and spirit of negotiation needed to accommodate diversity, and the relatively fluid yet nonetheless functional forms of trust and solidarity that emerge thereof to create what he terms a "dialogic democracy." Social movements, states Giddens (1994:120), contribute to this process of dialogic democracy by inserting "into the discursive domain aspects of social conduct that previously went undiscussed, or were 'settled' by traditional practices."

Seen in this light, alternative spiritual "magic" can be viewed as an informal, fluid, yet paradoxically unified social response to fundamentalisms of our time. By encouraging individual autonomy and tolerance for diversity, it is one of many contemporary venues for the promotion of dialogic democracy. As perhaps summarized by Giddens (1994:126):

> De Tocqueville spoke for many others when he portrayed a decline of communal responsibility in the face of coruscating egoism, a spectacle of isolated individuals "incessantly endeavoring to procure the petty and paltry pleasures with which they glut their lives." Egoism, however, should be distinguished from individuation, which neither stems from it nor (necessarily) leads to it. The advance of social reflexivity means that individuals have no choice but to make choices; and these choices define who they are. People have to "construct their own biographies" in order to sustain a coherent sense of self-identity. Yet they cannot do so without interacting with others and this very fact creates new solidarities. The key element here is the generating of trust, particularly via the transition to more active trust mechanisms.

In any event, explorations of alternative spirituality indicate the possibility of reconsidering not only distinctions between magic and religion, but the alleged differences between self- and socially-directed movements that underlie this distinction.

However, this is not to suggest that there cannot be limitations within the alternative spiritual milieu. As indicated in my analysis, ideological claims provide the individual with identity and meaning. Nonetheless, any ideological claim fundamentally is limited, even as it is often asserted as addressing the full range of life experience of the self (Simmel 1955; du Preez 1980; Cormack 1992). The accounts contained herein would hardly be an exception, given that there is a group ideology framing the account. As noted by Gusdorf (see Griffin 1990:152), "The task of autobiography is first of all a task of personal salvation," and such self-accounts discuss the protagonist not in terms of how he/she appears to the outside world, or necessarily how he/she truly "is," but rather who the given individual *believes or wishes to have been*. Such accounts, according to Gusdorf, represent "the effort of a creator to give the meaning of his own mythic tale."

In this context — indeed, in virtually any context — who one wishes to have been indicates social expectations beyond the self. Whether discussing one's countercultural spiritual development, or reasons for becoming a born-again Christian, getting a divorce, switching political parties, coming out as gay, and so forth, there are socioculturally accepted ways of telling one's story. One learns through observation and experience what factors to emphasize or omit so as to maximize or minimize certain underlying ideological claims inherent in the story being told. It would not be exaggerating to say that immersion in a particular belief system means learning how to articulate the ideology of this belief system. As Kerby (1991:45) states, "We already have language. We have been told stories, we have seen and read them; we are therefore no longer innocent in this respect. Our world is a progressively cultural one, where even nature is a cultural concept with a varying history."

Thus, socially located frameworks serve to create a self, but all creations are, by definition, limited; they are one thing and not another. The narratives chosen to be emphasized in one's story may feature biased aspects of self that serve to camouflage other, potentially productive aspects of self (Rosenwald and Ochberg 1992). Though they offer revelation, idealized or mythologized accounts also distort or block certain emotional urgencies. Therefore, the pull toward full integration of self can be obfuscated (Schneiderman 1981).

It is this dual function of virtually any ideology — to illuminate yet conceal — that may account for the collective ambivalence toward any one knowledge claim in our society. Whatever the system of belief, some will be drawn to its seeming power to explain, while others will be repelled by its seeming limitations. But since alternative spiritualism is somewhat at odds with dominant social forces, its limitations or paradoxes may seem more salient to some people than the limitations or paradoxes of mainstream, secular reasoning. While countercultural spiritual beliefs are gaining wider acceptance, doubtless there are many people who would not find it problematic for someone to say, "I felt bad about losing my job, but I talked to my minister and now I feel better," yet would find it problematic to hear someone say, "I felt bad about losing my job, but I talked to my Tarot teacher, and now I feel better."

In the meantime, alternative spirituality makes salient the underlying dilemmas in contemporary society over individuality and community, the sacred versus the secular, and the need for and limitations of ideology. Perhaps by studying such individuals, new information can be generated in regard to these paradoxes.

In sum, as with any other ideological claim, there were limits as to the utility or philosophical breadth of the comments made by interviewees. Nonetheless, interesting critiques of society appeared in the interviews, as well as interesting approaches to the dilemmas posed by contemporary society. If there are limits as to the utility or explanatory power of alternative spirituality, the same could and has been said of legitimized secular rationality. As Bales (1970:152) notes, life experience often is harsh, beyond the control or predictive skills of the individual. Ignorance of one form or another imposes constraints, and "with relatively little command over the energies of the physical world, it is easier to make moonshine than to move mountains."

NOTE

Excerpts from this chapter are forthcoming in a somewhat different form in *Journal for the Scientific Study of Religion* and *Review of Religious Research*.

Appendix A

The following provides a brief description of the various kinds of spirituality that are commonly referred to as forms of alternative spirituality.

Historically, "Paganism" (in the sense of polytheism) predates Christianity by centuries, but the technical label of "Pagan" probably dates back only as far as the early Middle Ages. The word "Pagan" meant "villager" — people who resided in villages were more likely to resist conversion to Christianity. Over the centuries, the term "Pagan" became associated with an absence of Judeo-Christian morality. Nonetheless, some understanding of these older religions survived through scholarship, in small pockets of believers, and sometimes in idiosyncratic expressions of an organized Christianity, in which the older religion and Christianity are homogenized. In the 1960s, aspects of these older beliefs and rituals seemed to speak to emergent hippie ideology, which helped create what is loosely termed "Neo-Paganism." One reason for a renewed interest in these older traditions (despite their many specific differences) was their tendency to embrace a wider range of organisms, objects and experience as sacred (Adler 1986; Starhawk 1987, 1989; Melton et al. 1990; Kelly 1992).

Numerous older religions can fall under the umbrella heading of "Neo-Paganism." Tribal shamanism — often Native American — has seen the advent of older traditions such as drumming, dancing, sacred fires, masks, and ritual sweats as popular tools and activities in countercultural spiritual circles. Often, these activities are enacted to invoke both an honoring of the earth (often imbued with a female divine nature, e.g., Mother Earth) and to hasten along one's spiritual/psychological development. The Greek or Hellenic canon has the advantage of familiarity, and might well have sparked some people's imaginations when as children they were exposed to the Greek deities and heroes. At festivals and events, I have met with Hellenic Neo-Pagans, but some people find the Greek tradition problematic for its alleged patriarchal elements. I have found that other general expressions of spirituality referred to as "Paganism" can include virtually any or all of the older European, Asian, African, Aboriginal, or Pan-American spiritual traditions. In fact, in defining "Neo-Paganism," Melton et al. (1990) refer to a somewhat similar multiplicity of spiritual traditions.

According to Melton et al. (1990), Wiccans — people who practice witchcraft — can be considered one expression of Neo-Paganism. Indeed, from interviews, lectures and conversations, I have found that "Wiccan" was sometimes used interchangeably with "Pagan" or "Neo-Pagan." However, not all people who associated with Neo-Paganism used witchcraft. Thus, while some people used the terms "Pagan," "Neo-Pagan," and "Wiccan" interchangeably, for others each term meant something specific — though not necessarily the same thing. In any event, Melton et al. (1990) point out that the Neo-Pagan individual is typified by a strong dislike for dogma, routinization and authority within their spiritual expression, which is why only a small percentage of Neo-Pagans belong or adhere to an organized body.

Goddess spirituality frequently draws upon Paganism or Wiccan belief systems, or both. Essentially, it seeks to emphasize and honor the feminine as a spiritual, cosmic force, whether through rituals of praise, or through the harnessing of this force to enact change or empowerment. There are women who find Goddess spirituality important in the articulation of their feminist stance (Adler 1986; Christ 1987; Starhawk 1987, 1989; Bednarowski 1991). Sometimes, these women organize all-female spiritual groups or circles to study and explore the power of the Goddess. There are also some men who pursue Goddess spirituality. However, some people (female or male) might participate in rituals, or read (and agree with) some of the literature that has been written on Goddess spirituality without labeling themselves "Goddess worshippers." Some people find the Goddess to be but one aspect of spiritual wholeness — albeit an important one that Christianity is viewed as having tried to destroy.

More so than the other labels listed in survey, "New Age" refers to a sense of personal development, and/or a generalized worldview that human society is "evolving" toward a new level of consciousness. What somewhat sets it apart from Neo-Paganism or Wicca is that there is more of a general ideology that people (often unconsciously) bring into their lives the challenges they need to develop as the godlike nature within the self, and so one should learn to accept one's fate as necessary spiritual growth, rather than enact conscious change — as through magic (Ferguson 1980; Melton and Moore 1982; Melton et al. 1990).

Another distinction between New Agers and Neo-Pagans is that the latter are less likely to believe in a unity of all religions, and more likely to see different deities of different religions as, in fact, different (Melton et al. 1990). Interestingly, Steven, the one individual in my sample who was involved in a rigorously Wiccan group felt this way. However, other people in my sample who engaged in at least some Neo-Pagan practices *did* believe that all religions potentially addressed the same underlying spiritual truths and/or deities.

In any event, some people I interviewed or spoke with informally maintained that the *actual* "difference" between New Age and Neo-Paganism was monetary. A common expression one heard went something like: "The difference between New Age and Neo-Paganism is a decimal point," referring to the general idea that if a Neo-Pagan event cost fifty dollars, a somewhat similar New Age event cost five hundred — or maybe even five thousand — dollars. As Melton et al. (1990) points out, in theory Neo-Pagans do not accept compensation for their spiritual acts, while New Agers do.

Nonetheless, an issue of *Llewellyn's New Worlds of Mind and Spirit* featured a shopping column of spiritual tools, music, and artifacts. The column was entitled "Connections of mind and Spirit: resources for the new age community" (Thorn 1995:23). However, the author of the column referred to his readers as "Pagans." In the same vein, I have met with people who were recognized as local spokespersons for the Neo-Pagan community (as it was likely to be called in the media), yet they did not personally label themselves as Neo-Pagan — or anything else.

In sum, it is useful and necessary for social scientists to attempt to make distinctions across these different forms of spirituality. But the people who actually practice these different forms of spirituality do not always make the same distinctions — or make any distinctions at all.

Appendix B

The following is the list of questions I asked each interviewee.

Part I: "There will be two parts to the interview. In the second part, I'll be asking you some specific questions, but now, in the first part, I'd like you to tell me the story of your spiritual journey. You can pause, you can change what you're saying in mid-sentence — that isn't what matters. I just want to hear you tell me your story in your own words."

(After the interviewee indicated that he/she was finished, specific questions are were asked of him/her, as per the notes I took.)

Part II: "Now I'm going to ask you the same questions I ask everyone. You might think that you've already talked about some of these things, but I'm going to ask them again, anyway."

1. What is your opinion of mainstream society?

2. What is your opinion of mainline religions?

3. What are your spiritual activities?

4. What are the sources of your spiritual information?

5. Do you ever meet people who share your beliefs?

6. Do you tell the story of your spiritual journey the same way to others as you have told it to me? Are there situations in which you would not share this story with others, and if so, what would they be?

7. If you had to summarize the story of your spiritual journey in once sentence, what would it be?

8. How would you evaluate your spiritual journey — is it a happy story, a sad story?

9. What does your spiritual journey mean to you right now, as of this moment?

10. One author I found talks about people having "identifying moments" that "touch the self directly" and suggest self-images that "spark sudden realizations [and] reveal hidden images of self." Have you ever had such an experience? If so, please describe it.

11. Does your daily life ever present you with challenges to your spiritual beliefs? If so, how do you go about trying to resolve these conflicts?

12. In your opinion, is there a difference between what people call "New Age" and "Neo-Paganism"? If so, what is the difference?

13. On the Consent Form you signed, I refer to "alternative spirituality," but I'm not sure I like that term. The people I interview all seem to have something in common spiritually, yet they also have different specific beliefs or practices that they follow. Do you think "alternative" is a good name for all of you? If not, can you think of a better word?

14. Now we're going to do some word associations. I'll say a word, and you tell me what comes to mind. You can say a lot after each word, you can say a little — it's up to you:
Goddess, God, earth, dualism, mythology, Native Americanism, ritual, magic, technology, evolution, darkness, synchronicity, dreams, tools, self, community, life.

15. What does it mean to be "on a spiritual path"?

16. If you were conducting these interviews instead of me, is there anything you would ask that I haven't asked?

17. Is there anything else you would like to add?

18. What is your age?

19. What is your occupation?

Bibliography

Adler, Margot. 1986. *Drawing Down the Moon: Witches, Druids, Goddess-Worshippers, and Other Pagans in America Today*. Boston: Beacon Press.

Albanese, Catherine L. 1992. "The Magical Staff: Quantum Healing in the New Age." Pp. 68-84 in *Perspectives on the New Age*, edited by J. R. Lewis and J. G. Melton. Albany, New York: State University of New York Press.

Allen, Paula G. 1992. *The Sacred Hoop: Recovering the Feminine in American Indian Traditions*. Boston: Beacon Press.

Bailey, Robert E., Jr. 1978. "Ethnography of Religious Factors in a Politically Oriented Communal Group of New England." Pp. 251-280 in *Community, Self and Identity*, edited by B. Misra and J. J. Preston. The Hague, Paris: Mouton Publishers.

Bales, Robert F. 1970. *Personality and Interpersonal Behavior*. New York: Holt, Rhinehart and Winston.

Baltazar, Eulalio R. 1973. *The Dark Center: A Process Theology of Blackness*. New York: Paulist Press.

Barker, Eileen. 1993. "Behold the New Jerusalems! Catch 22s in the Kingdom Building Endeavors of New Religious Movements." *Sociology of Religion* 54: 337-352.

Beckford, James A. 1989. *Religion and Advanced Industrial Society*. London: Unwin Hyman.

Bednarowski, Mary F. 1991. "Literature of the New Age: A review of representative sources." *Religious Studies Review* 17: 209-216.

Bellah, Robert N. 1976. "New Religious Consciousness and the Crisis in Modernity." Pp. 333-352 in *The New Religious Consciousness*, edited by C. Y. Glock and R. N. Bellah. Berkeley and Los Angeles: University of California Press.

Bennett, Gillian. 1986. "Narrative as Expository Discourse." *Journal of

American Folklore 99: 415-434.

Bourdieu, Pierre. 1984. *Distinction: A Social Critique of the Judgment of Taste.*
Cambridge: Harvard University Press.

——— .1994. "Rethinking the State: Genesis and Structure of the
Bureaucratic Field." *Sociological Theory* 12: 1-18.

Brewer, M. B. 1993. "Social Identity, Distinctiveness, and In-Group Homogeneity." *Social Cognition* 11 (1): 150-164.

Brown, Ed. 1995. "The Heart of the Kitchen: Coffee Meditation." *Shambhala Sun* 3 (6): 74-75.

Bruner, Jerome S. 1990. *Acts of Meaning.* Cambridge: Harvard University
Press.

Buechler, Steven M. 1995. "New Social Movement Theories." *The Sociological Quarterly* 36: 441-464.

Burke, Kenneth. 1989. *On Symbols and Society.* Chicago and London: The
University of Chicago Press.

Calhoun, Craig. 1994. "Social Theory and the Politics of Identity." Pp. 9-
36 in *Social Theory and the Politics of Identity*, edited by Craig Calhoun.
Cambridge, Massachusetts: Blackwell Publishers.

Campbell, Colin, and Shirley McIver. 1987. "Cultural Sources of Support
for Contemporary Occultism." *Social Compass* 34: 41-60.

Carter, Stephen L. 1993. *The Culture of Disbelief: How American Law and
Politics Trivialize Religious Devotion.* New York: Basic Books.

Christ, Carol P. 1987. *Laughter of Aphrodite: Reflections on a Journey to the
Goddess.* San Francisco: Harper & Row.

Cicero, Chic, and Sandra T. Cicero. 1995. "Self-Initiation: An Effective System for Spiritual Growth." *Llewellyn's New Worlds of Mind and Spirit*
(June/July) 953: 52-53.

Conway, D. J. 1995. "Friendly Familiars on Your Doorstep." *Llewellyn's
New Worlds of Mind and Spirit* (June/July): 10-12.

Cormack, Michael. 1992. *Ideology.* Ann Arbor, Michigan: The University of
Michigan Press.

Denzin, Norman K. 1989. *Interpretive Biography.* Newbury Park, California:
Sage.

Donahue, Michael J. 1993. "Prevalence and Correlates of New Age Beliefs
in Six Protestant Denominations." *Journal for the Scientific Study of Religion* 32 (2): 177-184.

du Preez, Peter. 1980. *The Politics of Identity: Ideology and the Human Image.*
Oxford: Basil Blackwell Publisher.

Durkheim, Emile. 1951. *Suicide: A Study in Sociology.* Glencoe, Illinois:
Free Press.

——— .1994. *The Elementary Forms of Religious Life.* New York: The Free
Press.

Engelsman, Joan C. 1987. "Beyond the Anima: The Female Self in the
Image of God." Pp. 93-106 in *Jung's Challenge to Contemporary Religion*,

edited by M. Stein and R. L. Moore. Wilmette, Illinois: Chiron Publications.

Eyer, S. 1995. "Orpheus in Orbit: Reframing Hellenistic Dualism of the Body and the Earth." *Green Egg: A Journal of the Awakening Earth* 28 (109): 4-6.

Fenn, Richard K. 1980. "Secular Constraints on Religious Language." *The Annual Review of the Social Sciences of Religion* 4: 61-83.

Ferguson, M. 1980. *The Aquarian Conspiracy : Personal and Social Transformation in the 1980s.* Los Angeles: J. P. Tarcher.

Gagnon, John H. 1992. "The Self, Its Voices, and Their Discord." Pp. 221-243 in *Investigating Subjectivity: Research on Lived Experience*, edited by C. Ellis and M. G. Flaherty. Newbury Park, California: Sage Publications.

Giddens, Anthony. 1994. *Beyond Left and Right: The Future of Radical Politics.* Stanford, California: Stanford University Press.

Gieryn, Thomas F. 1983. "Boundary-Work and the Demarcation of Science From Non-Science: Strains and Interests in Professional Ideologies of Science." *American Sociological Review* 48: 781-795

———.1988. "Distancing Science from Religion in Seventeenth-Century England." *Isis* 79: 582-93.

———.1995. "Boundaries of Science." Pp. 393-443 in *Handbook of Science and Technology Studies*, edited by S. Jasanoff, G. E. Markle, J. C. Petersen and T. Pinch. Thousand Oaks, California: Sage.

Gill, Sam. 1987. *Native American Religious Action: A Performance Approach to Religion.* Columbia, South Carolina: University of South Carolina Press.

Goode, W. J. 1951. *Religion Among the Primitives.* New York: Free Press.

Goodin, Robert E. 1992. *Green Political Theory.* Oxford: Polity Press.

"Green Egg Reader's Survey — Summer, 1995." *Green Egg: A Journal of the Awakening Earth* 28 (109): 39.

Griffin, Charles J. G. 1990. "The Rhetoric of Form in Conversion Narratives." *Quarterly Journal of Speech* 76: 152-163.

Griffin, Wendy. 1995. "The Embodied Goddess: Feminist Witchcraft and Female Divinity." *Sociology of Religion* 56: 35-48.

Gusfield, Joseph. 1981. "Social Movements and Social Change: Perspectives of Linearity and Fluidity." Pp. 317-339 in *Social Movements, Conflict and Change, Vol. 4.*, edited by L. Kreisberg. Greenwich, Connecticut: JAI Press.

———.1994. "The Reflexivity of Social Movements: Collective Behavior and Mass Society Theory Revisited." Pp. 58-78 in *New Social Movements: From Ideology to Identity*, edited by E. Larana, H. Johnston and J. Gusfield. Philadelphia: Temple University Press.

Harr, Rom. 1986. *Varieties of Realism: A Rationale for the Natural Sciences.* Oxford: Basil Blackwell.

Hess, David J. 1993. *Science in the New Age: The Paranormal, Its Defenders and Debunkers and American Culture.* Madison, Wisconsin: University of Wisconsin Press.

Hollway, Wendy. 1989. *Subjectivity and Method in Psychology: Gender, Meaning and Science.* London: Sage Publications.

Holton, Gerald J. 1993. *Science and Anti-Science.* Cambridge: Harvard University Press.

Houston, Siobhan. 1995. "Chaos Magic." *Gnosis: A Journal of the Western Inner Traditions* 36: 54-58.

Hultkrantz, Ake. 1987. *Native Religions of North America: The Power of Visions and Fertility.* San Francisco: Harper & Row.

Ingram, Catherine. 1995. "Teachers and Seekers: An Interview with Andrew Harvey." *Yoga Journal* (July/August) 123: 56-63.

Joy, W. B. 1993. "The Dark Awakening: Difficult Traverses in Spiritual Development." *Enlightenments: Reaching the Midwest, The Heart of America* (September): 22.

Juline, Kathy. 1995. "Architecture as Sacred Form: An Interview with Anthony Lawlor." *Science of Mind* 68 (8): 37-49.

Kanagy, Conrad L., and Hart M. Nelsen. 1995. "Religion and Environmental Concern: Challenging The Dominant Assumptions." *Review of Religious Research* 37 (1): 33-45.

Kelly, Aidan A. 1992. "An Update on Neo-Pagan Witchcraft in America." Pp. 136-151 in *Perspectives on the New Age*, edited by J. R. Lewis and J. G. Melton. Albany, New York: State University of New York Press.

Kerby, Anthony P. 1991. *Narrative and the Self.* Bloomington and Indianapolis: Indiana University Press.

Latour, Bruno. 1987. *Science in Action: How to Follow Scientists and Engineers through Society.* Cambridge: Harvard University Press.

Linde, Charlotte. 1993. *Life Stories: The Creation of Coherence.* New York and Oxford: Oxford University Press.

Longino, Helen E. 1990. *Science as Social Knowledge: Values and Objectivity in Scientific Inquiry.* Princeton: Princeton University Press.

Luckmann, Thomas. 1967. *The Invisible Religion.* New York: Macmillan.

Luhmann, Niklas. 1982. *The Differentiation of Society.* New York: Columbia University Press.

MacCormac, E. R. 1976. *Metaphor and Myth in Science and Religion.* Durham, North Carolina: Duke University Press.

Malinowski, Bronislaw. 1974. *Magic, Science and Religion.* London: Souvenir Press.

McCall, Michal M. 1990. "The Significance of Storytelling." Pp. 145-161 in *Studies in Symbolic Interaction*, Vol. II, edited by N. K. Denzin. Greenwich, Connecticut: JAI Press.

McGaa, Ed. 1992. *Rainbow Tribe: Ordinary People Journeying on the Red Road.* San Francisco: Harper.

McGuire, Meredith B. 1988. *Ritual Healing in Suburban America*. New Brunswick, New Jersey: Rutgers University Press.

Mead, George H. 1962. *Mind, Self and Society*. Chicago: University of Chicago Press.

Melton, J. Gordon, Jerome Clark, and Aidan A. Kelly. 1990. *New Age Encyclopedia*. Detroit and New York: Gale Research Inc.

Melton, J. Gordon, and Robert L. Moore. 1982. *The Cult Experience: Responding to the New Religious Pluralism*. New York: The Pilgrim Press.

Melucci, Alberto. 1985. "The Symbolic Challenge of Contemporary Movements." *Social Research* 52: 789-816.

———.1989. *Nomads of the Present: Social Movements and Individual Needs in Contemporary Society*. Philadelphia: Temple University Press.

———.1994. "A Strange Kind of Newness: What's 'New' In New Social Movements?" Pp. 101-130 in *New Social Movements: From Ideology to Identity*, edited by E. Larana, H. Johnston, and J. Gusfield. Philadelphia: Temple University Press.

Mishler, Elliot G. 1986. *Research Interviewing: Context and Narrative*. Cambridge, Massachusetts: Harvard University Press.

Misra, Bhabgrahi, and James J. Preston. 1978. "Introduction." Pp. 1-6 in *Community, Self and Identity*, edited by B. M. and J. J. Preston. The Hague and Paris: Mouton Publishers.

Neitz, Mary Jo. 1994. "Quasi-Religions and Cultural Movements: Contemporary Witchcraft as a Churchless Religion." Pp. 127-149 in *Religion and the Social Order*, Vol. 4, edited by A. L. Greil and T. Robbins. Greenwich, Connecticut: JAI Press.

Oliver, Joan D. 1996. "Images For the Soul." *New Age Journal* (August): 88-93.

Proudfoot, Wayne. 1977. "Religious Experience, Emotion, and Belief." *The Harvard Theological Review* 70: 343-367.

———.1985. *Religious Experience*. Berkeley and Los Angeles: University of California Press.

Riessman, C. K. 1990. *Divorce Talk: Women and Men Make Sense of Personal Relationships*. New Brunswick and London: Rutgers University Press.

———.1993. *Narrative Analysis*. Newbury Park, California and London: Sage Publications.

Roof, Wade C. 1985. "The Study of Social Change in Religion." Pp. 75-89 in *The Sacred in a Secular Age: Toward Revision in the Scientific Study of Religion*, edited by P. E. Hammond. Berkeley and Los Angeles: The University of California Press.

Rosenwald, George C., and Richard L. Ochberg. 1992. "Introduction: Life Stories, Cultural Politics, and Self-Understanding." Pp. 1-18 in *Storied Lives: The Cultural Politics of Self-Understanding*, edited by G. C. Rosenwald and R. L. Ochberg. New Haven and London: Yale University Press.

Schneiderman, Leo. 1981. *The Psychology of Myth, Folklore and Religion.* Chicago: Nelson-Hall.

Shotter, John. 1993. *Conversational Realities: Constructing Life Through Language.* London: Sage Publications.

Simmel, Georg. 1955. *Conflict and The Web of Group Affiliations.* New York: The Free Press.

Smoley, Richard. 1995. "Editorial." *Gnosis: A Journal of the Western Inner Traditions,* 36: 1.

Somers, Margaret R., and Gloria D. Gibson. 1994. "Reclaiming the Epistemological 'Other': Narrative and the Social Construction of Identity." Pp. 37-99 in *Social Theory and the Politics of Identity,* edited by C. Calhoun. Cambridge, Massachusetts: Blackwell Publishers.

———. 1989. *The Spiral Dance: A Rebirth of the Religion of the Great Goddess.* New York: Harper and Row.

———.1987. *Truth or Dare: Encounters with Power, Authority and Mystery.* Starhawk. San Francisco: Harper.

Stone, Donald. 1978. "New Religious Consciousness and Personal Religious Experience." *Sociological Analysis* 39: 123-134.

Stromberg, Peter G. 1993. *Language and Self-Transformation: A Study of the Christian Conversion Narrative.* Cambridge: Cambridge University Press.

Swartz, Paul. 1985. "Of Time and Personal Myth." *Perceptual and Motor Skills* 6: 1207-1214.

Szuchewycz, Bohdan. 1994. "Evidentiality in Ritual Discourse: The Social Construction of Religious Meaning." *Language in Society* 23: 389-410.

Thorn, Michael. 1995. "Connections of Mind and Spirit: Sacred Shopping." *Llewellyn's New Worlds of Mind and Spirit* 953: 23-25.

Titiev, Mischa. 1972. "A Fresh Approach to the Problem of Magic and Religion." Pp. 430-433 in *Reader in Comparative Religion: An Anthropological Approach,* edited by W. A. Lessa and E. Z. Vogt. New York: Harper and Row.

Travers, Peter L. 1975. "Myth, Symbol and Tradition." Pp. 111-124 in *Sacred Tradition and Present Need,* edited by J. Needleman and D. Lewis. New York: The Viking Press.

Turner, Ralph H. 1976. "The Real Self: From Institution to Impulse." *American Journal of Sociology* 81: 989-1016

Volosinov, V. N. 1973. *Marxism and the Philosophy of Language.* New York: Seminar Press.

White, Timothy. 1995. "Pray for the Water, Pray for the Land: An Interview with Western Shoshone Elder, Corbin Harney." *Shaman's Drum: A Journal of Experiential Shamanism* 38: 30-39.

Wuthnow, Robert. 1976. "The New Religions in Social Context." Pp. 267-294 in *The New Religious Consciousness,* edited by C. Y. Glock and R. N. Bellah. Berkeley and Los Angeles: University of California Press.

———.1985. "Science and the Sacred." Pp. 187-203 in *The Sacred in a Secular Age: Toward Revision in the Scientific Study of Religion*, edited by P. E. Hammond. Berkeley and Los Angeles: University of California Press.

———.1994. *Sharing the Journey: Support Groups and America's New Quest for Community*. New York: Free Press.

Young, K. G. 1987. *Taleworlds and Storyrealms: The Phenomenology of Narrative*. Dordrecht, The Netherlands: Martinus Nijhoff Publishers.

Zurcher, Louis A. 1983. *Social Roles: Conformity, Conflict and Creativity*. Beverly Hills: Sage.

Index

About the Author

JON P. BLOCH is Assistant Professor of Sociology at Southern Connecticut State University. His research and teaching interests include social theory, sociology of religion, and sociology of sex and gender.

ISBN 0-275-95957-0

HARDCOVER BAR CODE